THE
HAUNTED
HEART OF
AMERICA

About the Author

Dr. Logan Corelli has been studying and investigating the paranormal for over seventeen years. He is a parapsychologist, metaphysician, and director of a paranormal investigation team. He has led several other paranormal teams over the years and worked with many more to investigate and collect evidence of paranormal activity. He holds a PhD in parapsychology and a doctorate in metaphysics as well as his parapsychologist certification and other paranormal-related certifications. Through the years, he has hosted and participated in several paranormal conventions, conferences, and ghost tours, including one to raise money to preserve and save an old historic building.

Corelli has made many TV appearances throughout the years, including several episodes of Animal Planet's *The Haunted* and many local news segments about haunted locations. He was including in the filming of *Ghosts and Legends of Oklahoma* and is currently filming his own TV series entitled *Paranormal America*, which will feature haunted locations from all over the United States. He has been published in several newspapers and magazines with stories of local haunts and investigations, including many historical sites. He is also an ordained reverend and has some experience with exorcism.

Corelli also enjoys cooking, photography, and doing video work with various projects. He currently lives in one of his childhood homes, which has been haunted at times, in Midwest City, Oklahoma. Should you want to contact him, please email him directly at Loganokcgc@yahoo.com.

LOGAN CORELLI

THE
HAUNTED
HEART OF
AMERICA

In-Depth Investigations of the Villisca Ax Murder House,
Myrtles Plantation & Other Frightful Sites

Llewellyn Publications
Woodbury, Minnesota

FIRST EDITION
First Printing, 2018

Cover design by Kevin R. Brown
Interior photos courtesy of the author

Llewellyn Publications is a registered trademark of Llewellyn Worldwide Ltd.

Library of Congress Cataloging-in-Publication Data (Pending)
ISBN: 978-0-7387-5591-5

Llewellyn Worldwide Ltd. does not participate in, endorse, or have any authority or
responsibility concerning private business transactions between our authors and the public.

All mail addressed to the author is forwarded but the publisher cannot, unless specifically
instructed by the author, give out an address or phone number.

Any internet references contained in this work are current at publication time, but the
publisher cannot guarantee that a specific location will continue to be maintained. Please
refer to the publisher's website for links to authors' websites and other sources.

Llewellyn Publications
A Division of Llewellyn Worldwide Ltd.
2143 Wooddale Drive
Woodbury, MN 55125-2989
www.llewellyn.com

Printed in the United States of America

For Danae and Ashley

Contents

INTRODUCTION

You come home late one night exhausted from a long day at work. You throw your keys down on the kitchen table and start down the long hallway to the bedroom. Suddenly, you hear a noise behind you and stop. It is the sound of someone dragging their feet across the carpet. You look, but no one can be seen. An arctic air blows past you just as you look over and see a massive shadowy figure standing next to you. Then you feel the cold brush of a hand grab your arm. You spin around to confront your attacker, only to find no one is there. You hear the distant sound of a door in the house slamming shut just as the room returns to normal.

This is one of the many different types of paranormal encounters that literally thousands of people across the United States experience in their lifetime. Explanations for these encounters are what bring me to locations and the people that experience them. For almost two decades I have been seeking out paranormal activity for research and documentation purposes as well as helping people understand and live with whatever may be residing in their home with them. It's never easy for someone to hear that their home or place of business is inhabited by spirits. Most would flee just from the idea that there are invisible invaders watching them at every turn. Some, however, flock to those locations and wait for a supernatural encounter.

With the popularity of ghosts and the paranormal today, there has been a huge demand for genuine haunted locations. Throughout the country, haunted hotels, businesses, and abandoned buildings are open to the public for tours and overnight stays to anyone interested in having a paranormal experience. However, many people don't have to even leave the house to have experiences, as they're living in their very own haunted house. But what exactly is a haunted house? Some can drive through a neighborhood, look at a house, and say, "That house is haunted." But it takes more than a dark and creepy-looking old house to make it haunted. Most houses have paranormal activity that is not the "run out of the house screaming for your life" type. In fact, the activity is sometimes so subtle that without proper investigation, you would never know it was haunted. There are those few-and-far-between cases, however, that have more extreme activity, and a few of them are documented in this book.

Throughout the course of this book, I will be walking you through some of the most memorable and fascinating cases I have been on and the evidence I have collected from them. A few of them are some of the most haunted locations throughout the United States and have had activity recorded and experienced by visitors for many years. The entire content of this book will be written through my perspective as the events are taking place. This is not an official report or case log, but simply my own personal diary of each location visited.

Before we begin, I feel it is necessary to tell you a little bit about myself, my history with the paranormal, and how I became involved with parapsychology. At a very young age I was exposed to paranormal activity and what I now believe to be spiritual encounters. Being as educated as I am today, I can better understand some of those experiences with the supernatural, but still to this day many of them remain unexplained.

The first extreme encounter I had with the paranormal was when I was just eight years old. My mother and I had vacationed at a resort in eastern Oklahoma. On the long trip home, we stopped at the Fountainhead Lodge, a lodge unlike anything I had ever seen before. The building was huge and rounded. We pulled up to the building, gathered our things, and headed inside.

The first thing that was to frighten me was when my mother asked me to go down the hallway to the ice machine and fill the ice bucket. Our room was at one end of the floor, and the ice machine was all the way at the other end. I made my approach to the ice machine and gathered the ice. As I started back, I paused and looked back toward the machine. There was a shadow of a figure on the wall directly across from it. The shadow appeared to be a silhouette of a slim man just under six feet tall. I started walking back to the room, kept looking back, and noticed when I started to walk, the shadow started taking small steps in my direction to follow me, only at a slower pace. I kept turning back around occasionally to see if it was still moving. I looked back only to see the shadow had stopped. I took a few more steps then stopped as well. Then it broke into a run right toward me.

I took off toward the room. When I finally made it to the door, I threw the bucket on the floor, which caused the ice to tumble all over the carpet as if someone burst open a bag of marbles. I started banging frantically on the door and yelling for my mother to open it and let me back in. I backed up against the hotel room door and waited for whatever was going to happen. The running shadow made its way to me, and when it was exactly across from me cowering in front of the door, it dissipated in almost a smoke-like way. My mother eventually opened the door, and I fell on the floor in the doorway of the room. She looked down at me and the ice spilled on the carpet floor.

As I told my mother the story of the phantom, she laughed at me and said, "You should have better things to do than chase your own shadow down the hall." She told me to get up and go get more ice from the machine. I politely refused. She picked up the ice bucket from the floor in the hallway and walked down the hall to get it herself.

Later that night, there were three loud knocks on the door. My mother checked the peep hole and saw no one outside. She opened the door slightly and said, "That was strange," as she closed and relocked it. About ten minutes later, the three loud knocks manifested again. My mother once again checked the hallway, only to find it void of any human occupants.

After this series of knocks, she decided to hide behind the door where she could not be seen and as soon as the door knocks happened, she would open the door immediately. She stood behind the door and, sure enough, the knocks came. She grabbed the door and jumped into the hallway. There was no one there by the door and no one in the hallway. She took a few steps back into the doorway of room and stood by the door, holding it open with her left hand. As the door stood open and my mother gazed into the hallway, a series of louder knocks came upon the door as she held it open.

We again huddled to the back of the room. Then, suddenly, we could hear a distant wind howling. Eventually, the wind had escalated to the point that the windows were almost shaking back and forth. The outside environment, however, was totally calm. The trees were not moving nor was anything being blown around. After about five to ten minutes of this, it stopped. Then, out of nowhere, the window started to fog up in a twelve-by-twelve-inch square on the window glass. I then discovered that the "fog" was on the outside of the window. The very last thing I remembered seeing in that room was the blank patch of fog there and seeing the words *you're dead* slowly appear in the fog. The activity was convincing enough for us to leave for the evening.

Eventually, I grew tired of experiencing these things and not knowing anything about them. I started my research into the paranormal just out of high school. Growing up, I had always watched TV shows and read books about the paranormal. When the internet was introduced, I found it a valuable asset for furthering my research into the paranormal. After several years of book and internet research, I began going out on investigations to try and capture evidence of the afterlife. When I had first started, I was armed with only an EMF detector, a 35mm camera, an audio recorder, a flashlight, and several books on the paranormal that guided me in collecting evidence. Today, I have much more advanced equipment to help me investigate the paranormal, including audio and video tools.

Over the past seventeen years I have had the privilege of being part of numerous paranormal teams, including those I started myself. Now, I am the director/leader of a small group that I run locally and work closely with a few local individuals as well as professionals in the field. I have met many great people and made numerous friends in the field as well as fell in love with one of the most amazing and beautiful women in the world. I have also had the chance to work with several TV productions, magazines, and newspapers.

It is my goal and passion to educate the public about the paranormal and related phenomena as well as share my experiences with them in the process. Most people have a common misunderstanding about the paranormal, and I want to be one to show them the reality of the phenomena. I will be including some of the history and stories about each location along with my own experiences to provide background on why the place may or may not be haunted. I will be documenting all anomalous activity as well as personal impressions. Let me explain a few things that you will encounter in this book that you might find questionable.

First, all the experiences I have documented are true. None of the information or stories has been fabricated or exaggerated for this book. Some of the stories you might find unbelievable, but I can assure you all the events happened and all the evidence is real. Next, all my theories about the paranormal and investigative methods are my own. I don't follow a specific guideline for investigations. I utilize several pieces of equipment used by parapsychologists around the world and document their readings. When you read through this book, you might find several things I do questionable, but please keep in mind that I have reasoning for my actions, most of which will be explained.

I hope you will find this book entertaining as well as educational. I took great pleasure in conducting these investigations. I'm not trying to convince you of anything—I ask only that you keep an open mind when reading and draw your own conclusions. I chose these locations not just for their past reputation for being haunted, but also for their power to convince even the strongest of skeptics to believe that the existence of the paranormal is possible. With that said, let us begin.

Chapter 1

THE ST. JAMES HOTEL

Cimarron, New Mexico

Tucked away in the northeast portion of New Mexico is the town of Cimarron. It's a mountainous and secluded area of the state that is peaceful as well as historic. It's not the town nor the history, however, that attracts so many people to the area—it's the haunted St. James Hotel. The St. James Hotel has had years of fame and notoriety not only for being an Old Western landmark, but also for the spirits that dwell within it and have made many guests over the years fascinated with as well as believers in ghosts. It was 1872 when Henri Lambert established the St. James Saloon in Cimarron, New Mexico. Lambert, who was the personal chef to President Abraham Lincoln, converted the saloon to a hotel in 1880. The hotel was visited by many famous lawmen and outlaws over the years. Wyatt Earp, Jesse James, and Annie Oakley were just a few of the famous Wild West figures to stay at the St. James.

It was the history of spirits that landed me on the St. James Hotel's doorstep. I had seen several television shows about the paranormal events that took place in the hotel, and it sparked my interest. I researched information on the internet about the hotel and its reported activity and learned that there had been a few paranormal investigation teams that had visited the hotel over the years and yielded many results. It was obvious from the experiences and investigations that something, or rather someone, remained over the years in the St. James as a guest. Numerous spirits are said to haunt this old historic hotel, but who exactly are they? Well, let's look at the suspects.

The St. James Hotel.

One of the most famous and notorious ghosts said to roam the halls of the hotel is that of a man named Thomas J. "TJ" Wright. His spirit is said to linger in room 18, which is kept padlocked even to this day. The supposed history behind his death is that one day TJ won possession of the hotel in a card game. The owner was reluctant to turn the ownership over so easily. Guns were drawn and TJ was shot. He dragged himself down the hallway to what is now room 18 and expired. When I inquired about why the room was locked, I was told that the previous owners had been attacked by a swirling white light in the room and kept the door locked to keep the spirit contained. Contain a spirit? Can they be serious? I believe it was more of a deal that was made in which the owners would keep people out of his room if he agreed not to disturb or harm any of the guests. I remember hearing another story about the room that wasn't told by the building owners. A reporter from a TV show had visited the hotel many years ago in hopes of documenting the story and the phenomena. When the crew was inside room 18, one of the cameramen made a crude remark about the spirit being in the room, and an unseen force flung the reporter across the room. Needless to say, they never returned and the story never aired.

Another famous spirit (and probably the most frequently seen and heard) of the hotel is that of Mary Lambert. Mary, who was the wife of the building's founder, Henri, is said to come into room 17 late at night if the window is open and tap on it until the window is shut. She has also materialized in brief moments: visitors of the room see a quick image of a woman moving about the room late at night. Mary likes to make her presence known in the room by the smell of her floral perfume. The overwhelming scent can overpower even the strongest smells in the room, but no source of the scent has ever been found.

Other spirits seen in the hotel include an old man named "Little Imp" and a small child with a burned face who has been seen sitting on the bar late at night spinning a glass. Most of these spirits haunt the bar area of the hotel on the first floor.

First Investigation:
Missing Water and Found Underwear

After researching this information and months of preparation, I set out to experience the phenomena for myself. In August 2005, I traveled the eight hours from Midwest City, Oklahoma, to Cimarron, New Mexico, for the first time in hopes of documenting (and experiencing) the activity that had so long been reported. Tyrone, a personal friend and experienced paranormal investigator, accompanied me on this journey to help perform and document the investigation.

We arrived at the hotel and unpacked everything. We were to stay two nights at the hotel in room 17, which was Mary's room. The room was fairly small, almost the size of a standard bedroom, with one bed and a bathroom. We decided to have dinner in the hotel restaurant due to the late hour and not knowing the area well enough to go venturing out at dark. After dinner, we escorted a few guests around the hotel, answering questions about the paranormal and taking readings and pictures in their rooms. When we returned to room 17, we decided to leave the window open for Mary Lambert to see if we could get the tapping to occur. It did not. Throughout the night, we did, however, smell the overwhelming perfume in the room.

The second day began like any other. We went down to the restaurant and had breakfast. As we ate, we discussed the plan of operation for the night's investigation. A couple that was staying in the hotel volunteered to take us on a tour of an old cemetery that was up on the mountain. We drove up to the mountain and made the short hike up to the ruins of an old cemetery that appeared to have been abandoned for some time. Seeing no ghosts or snakes, we decided to head back to the hotel and start the setup for the investigation.

Late the second night, we were in our room talking about the plans for the night's investigation and how it appeared as if the activity was extremely low for an investigation. Earlier that day, after taking a bath, I was having problems with the water draining out of the bathtub. I didn't feel like bothering with it, so I left it alone and said nothing to the management. During our conversation about the night's investigation, I walked into the bathroom to use it. As I stood there, I looked at the water still sitting in the tub. Disappointed, I walked out of the room and said to my friend, "If there are any spirits here, tell them to go in the bathroom and drain the water out of the tub so I can take another bath."

Approximately fifteen minutes later, my friend went into the bathroom to use it and said, "Hey, did you let the water out of the tub?"

"No, the drain is still clogged," I said. He told me that the water was no longer in the bathtub. In disbelief, I walked into the bathroom and the tub was empty and dry. We did not hear any water drain out of the tub and have no idea where the water had gone. Also, even if the water had drained out, the tub should not have been totally dry.

Perplexed, we continued with the night's investigation. We made a trip downstairs to the hotel bar and lobby area to set up some equipment. The only activity we had was a small spike activation on one of our electromagnetic field (EMF) detectors. These EMF detectors are used to indicate possible paranormal activity by measuring electromagnetic fields, which could indicate the presence of a spirit manifesting or moving through

a particular area. Once we were finished, we headed back upstairs and visited the poker room where TJ was shot. On our
way down the hall, we stopped in front of room 18. My friend
was whispering very provoking things at the door in hopes of
getting something to happen. Just after he was finished talking,
there was a vibration that came from the floor below. I had to
move over to the door to see for myself, and there was indeed a
small vibration right in front of the door and nowhere else in
the hall. We could not conclude that the vibrating of the floor
was indeed paranormal and could not properly examine it either. If it was the spirit of TJ Wright, I guess he wasn't in the
mood for games that night. I was told that the owners of the
building used to leave a bottle of whiskey next to the bed for
him but wasn't told if he ever drank any of it.

The next day we got up and decided to start packing up on
the way home. While we were packing, my friend noticed a pair
of women's underwear that appeared on his pile of equipment;
he referred to them as "granny panties." They looked very old
fashioned and worn. He asked if I knew anything about them,
but I said no. We left them in the corner for the maid and
started our trip back to Oklahoma.

The trip was not very eventful or conclusive as we did not
hear the tapping on the window in our room, nor did we capture any photographic evidence or electronic voice phenomena
(EVP). EVP are classified as voices of spirits that are captured
on video or audio devices. We did have some personal experiences, such as the floor boards vibrating, but nothing too exciting. My second trip, however, was not the same.

Second Investigation: The Bar and the Bathroom

Over the course of the next six months, I could not get the St. James out of my head. I knew it wouldn't be long before I had the opportunity to go back, and I wanted to take full advantage of it. I also knew that when I returned, I would need more team members and more equipment to perform a better, more thorough investigation. In addition, I knew at this time of year the hotel would not be overly swarming with guests and we would have a great opportunity to collect some good data.

In April of 2006, I made my return to the hotel. Three team members accompanied me on this trip, one of whom was Brandon, a video guru. When we arrived at the hotel, we unpacked and headed to eat. Brandon and I stayed in room 17 (the Mary Lambert Room), and the other two investigators, Albert and Penny, stayed in room 20 (the Annie Oakley Room).

When we returned from eating, I ventured down the hallway to the poker room. We needed to film re-creation shots for a video documentary of the St. James we were putting together for our group. We did this on several investigations to document our experiences there. I stayed for about five minutes moving chairs around and started my way back down the hallway toward our room.

As I approached the corner to turn, I heard footsteps heading toward the same corner from the other direction. Trying to avoid a collision, I stopped and stepped to the side to let the other individual go by me. The footsteps reached the end of the corner and beyond, but no one appeared. I approached the corner halfway expecting someone to jump out and try to scare me. I stuck my head around the corner and the hallway was empty. I knew the floor was so creaky that if anyone would have run off, I would have heard them. Also, if someone would have gone into a room, I would have heard the door open and close. I knew it could not have been my own footsteps I was hearing around the corner because when I stopped walking, the footsteps continued about three or four more steps. I went downstairs and told the gang about my experience, and we proceeded with our preparation of the night's investigation.

The poker room in the St. James Hotel.

We broke out all the equipment and started checking everything. We were fortunate to have met up with two young women who agreed to let us research their room and tagged along with us for the investigation. The women were staying in room 16, which was the Jesse James Room. We spent about forty-five minutes in room 16 with no positive results other than a few noises that we heard in the hallway. The noises, however, were not deter-

mined to be paranormal in nature. The rest of the investigations went pretty much the same way, with no conclusive data.
The other two investigators decided to go to bed and agreed to
meet us for breakfast the next morning in the restaurant downstairs.

Brandon and I were not tired and started thinking of something to do for the remainder of the evening. We started our
venture in the poker room. Inside the room, there was an
old-fashioned Ouija board on the table. The room was small,
with a chandelier and several chairs surrounding the small table. It was hard to imagine a large poker game being held here,
but I'm sure long ago they had to make do with it. We sat down,
and I jokingly asked Brandon if he wanted to try it out and see
if "anyone" was in the room. Now, let me say that I don't con-
done the use of a Ouija board for spiritual or paranormal investigative reasons, but we were bored and I thought Brandon
would enjoy it, seeing that he had very little experience and
knowledge of it. We both placed a hand on the planchette (a
piece of plastic used to find letters to answer) and asked if there
was anyone here with us. The planchette moved to *yes*.

We asked, "What is your name?" The board spelled out the
letters *R-U*. We didn't know if those were initials or if it was short
for a name (Rupert, Russell, etc.). The board never specified.

We then asked, "Did you die here?" The board pointed to *yes*.
"When?" *1875*.

Just to see if Brandon was manipulating the planchette, I
would periodically move my hand away from the piece. It would
slightly move on its own and stop, so I knew there was no way
Brandon or I could influence where the indicator went.

Last, we asked, "What keeps you here?" The board spelled
out a strange series of letters that we didn't understand.

Brandon asked, "What does that mean?" The board promptly spelled out the word *death*. We looked at each other, decided it was time to stop experimenting with the board, said goodbye, and exited the poker room.

Thinking of where to head next, we made our way down to the lobby. We looked around at all the brochures and pamphlets about the hotel and the antiques that were cased in glass, including some newspaper articles about the haunted history and ghosts of the hotel. Brandon then stopped and said, "I don't understand something; if the hotel was built in 1880, there is no way RU could have died here if the place wasn't in existence." The sign on the outside of the hotel read "St. James Hotel, 1880."

Then it clicked. The St. James was built in 1872 as a saloon and established as a hotel in 1880. RU could have died during the saloon period from a bar fight or shoot-out. They never specified how they met their end. It was, however, possible that the spirit (if that is what we were communicating with) did die at the hotel in 1875.

We finished looking in the lobby and talked about our next move. I had told him the story of the bar and the little boy seen on the bar spinning the glass. We decided to move into the bar and learn what we could hear or see. On our way, we walked through the dining room. I always felt this was an interesting room due to the bullet holes in the ceiling from the long-gone days of the Wild West. I often wondered if the holes still held the bullets, seeing that there was the slim possibility that some of them could still be in the wall, but I never got around to asking. Every time I walked into the room when it was dark, I got an interesting feeling, like there were people sitting at the tables watching my every move. I would stop for a minute or two every time I passed to try to communicate with anyone who could be in there but never got a response.

As we entered the bar area, I had the strangest feeling. There was very strong energy present, and I knew that something or someone was down there with us. They were hiding and did not want to be seen, at least not yet. We sat at the bar and Brandon lit up a cigarette. We started talking about the area and the "electrical" field that seemed to surround the bar. He asked which glass the child was spinning on the bar and I pointed up to one.

"Should we put the glass on the bar to see if it triggers any type of activity?" Brandon asked. I agreed, and he proceeded to walk around the bar and stopped about halfway back. He started backing up really slowly.

"What's the matter?" I asked.

He said he was dizzy and a very strong electrical field came over him when he walked around the bar, and he needed to sit down. We both took a seat at the bar and started asking questions to see if we could get a reaction or response. At one point, we got up and walked around the bar and dining room.

"I saw a figure pass in front of the doorway to the main kitchen area," Brandon told me. As he was explaining what the shadow looked like, we started hearing noises coming from the room behind the bar. We both stood in front of the bar area to listen.

A sudden loud clacking noise shot across the floor from behind the bar. We both jumped back very suddenly, and when we did, we both experienced a very high electrical sensation, like walking into an electric fence. The feeling happened for about two seconds and ceased. We looked at each other and confirmed what we had both just experienced. At that point, we were both feeling tired and had enough for the night and started back to our room.

When we entered the room, we hit the lights and went to bed. Lying there, I started looking around the room curiously, and my attention focused on the ceiling. I saw a relatively large shadowy figure in the upper corner of the room above the door. It would change or shift periodically. Normally, I would look to the window to find something outside was causing the shadow (in most cases a tree, which would move due to wind). This was not the case due to there being no trees around the area of the hotel, and the room was on the second floor. I then noticed the form had what appeared to be a long, slender arm pointing. I looked in the direction it was pointing and noticed another large shadow mass. This one did not change in any way. I asked Brandon to verify that what I was seeing was accurate and that I wasn't just seeing things. He confirmed seeing the same thing.

We then heard tapping on the open window followed by eerie scratching down the glass. This occurred several times throughout the night, but the most bizarre event I had ever experienced at the St. James Hotel was soon to follow.

The room was extremely dark and quiet. I started looking around the room, waiting to fall asleep. We had left the bathroom door open, and I focused my attention there. I almost immediately saw a faint face come out of the darkness and stare directly at us. Along with the face was an arm that was waving us to come into the bathroom. The arm would appear and disappear several times. I did not know if I was the only one able to see this or if anyone could. I also had to have confirmation that I did not fall asleep and was dreaming. I turned and asked Brandon to look into the bathroom.

He immediately retreated under the covers as if something scared him. I asked him what he saw, and he said to me the only thing he saw was the whites of someone's eyes floating in the bathroom. I asked him to look again. He was a little reluctant, but he again looked into the bathroom and again took refuge under the covers.

"It's important. You need to tell me what you're seeing," I told him.

This time he said he had seen the actual face of a person looking back at him. I told him to look again. After some hesitation, he made a third glance at the dark bathroom and saw the hand that was waving us into the bathroom. He then decided he had seen enough and rolled over to go to sleep. I stayed lying there looking at the faint form that kept beckoning us into the bathroom. Eventually the room became blurry as I drifted off to sleep.

When we woke the next morning, I made a tour around the room and the bathroom to see if anything was out of place or different. I took a quick EMF sweep of the bathroom to find no readings. We met with the other two investigators for breakfast and to tell them what had happened the night before. It turns out Albert had a story to tell us as well. He asked if we went to sleep okay and if we had any trouble sleeping. We explained what had happened with the form on the ceiling and the figure in the bathroom.

In return, he told us that his wife, Penny, had no trouble falling asleep, and he was almost asleep when he experienced a bizarre incident he could not explain: he heard this woman screaming right beside his head. It was very mechanical sounding and repetitive. He sat up to look around but did not see anything unusual. He tried again to fall asleep and the incident reoccurred. He had heard the woman's voice several times throughout the night, and it was always when he was just about to sleep.

The room they were staying in, which was Annie Oakley's room, had a history of activity. I had heard a story about the room on my previous trip. I heard that the spirit in that room (more than likely female) liked to unpack women's clothes and scatter them about the room. The men's clothes however would remain neatly folded and untouched. Could this be the work of a jealous female spirit that inhabits the room? There was no way to tell for sure. Perhaps the spirit wanted Albert to stay awake while Penny was asleep. There was no evidence collected, so we had nothing to prove one way or another. I was interested in the event mainly because I felt that the investigator had made a connection with the spirit, which we could use for the next night's investigation.

On the second night, the activity was not as active as the first. We were filming a reenactment of the TJ Wright shooting for the documentary video we were putting together and decided to take a break from filming to go eat. We had placed the modern chairs against the wall so they would not be in the shot of the film and left. When we returned, one of the modern chairs was placed right back up against the table where it had been originally. We were the only ones in the entire hotel, and I couldn't imagine anyone else going into that room to place the chair at the table. However, we did not have a camera set up to monitor the area, so we could not conclude it was something paranormal.

Brandon and I were shooting video at the base of the stairs to wait for the midnight hour when the grandfather clock would make its final strikes, indicating the next day. Brandon felt it would be a good for the video, so we positioned the camera accordingly.

Midnight came and the clock slammed out its twelve strokes. An eerie feeling overcame the hotel at that moment. I looked down the hallway in both directions. It felt as though the energy level were increasing around the environment. I told Brandon that the clock could have been a summoning device for the spirits to "come out and play." Having the video clip, we continued with the investigation. We tried desperately to get the events of the previous night to reoccur in the bar but with no success. No sound, EVP, or photographic evidence was captured. We continued investigating the rest of the hotel through the night and eventually retired to our room.

Several times throughout the night as we tried to go to sleep, Brandon and I heard footsteps walking up and down the hallway and stairs. We knew the other investigators were in their room and would not be pacing the stairs up and down at three o'clock in the morning. Also, these were not normal shoes. It sounded more to me like a heavy boot, as the sound was loud and obvious. I had also heard a female voice come from inside the room. The bathroom remained empty and quiet, and we eventually fell asleep. The next day we packed our things and started our long venture back home.

Third Investigation: The Last Visit

I made one more trip to the hotel. One of the big differences between this last trip the others is that I had twice as many people with me on the investigation. This can be a good or bad thing: good because this allows us to take more equipment, which lets us gather more documented readings and more evidence to analyze; and bad, because with so many people around, whatever

might be there is more likely to avoid us as a group and possibly interact more when we are split up. Nothing is certain,
but I thought it was going to be an interesting trip. This time
I hoped that the hotel was going to be the most active it's ever
been and that we could get some conclusive evidence that the St.
James had some invisible guests staying there. It was March 17,
2007, and it was time ro enter the doors of the St. James Hotel
one last time.

I decided to take this trip with Ashley, my girlfriend at the
time, and members of another team. There were six of us in
total that would be going. We made a ritual stop in Amarillo
to eat lunch. (I always managed to stop at the Big Texan Steak-
house due to the good food and atmosphere.) We also stopped
at a highway gas station near Cimarron and a local grocery
store for snacks and fuel. Ashley and I were the first to arrive at
the hotel, so we decided to check in and wait for the rest of the
group to arrive.

We received a phone call from the other team informing us
that they were delayed due to travel issues but would be arriving
shortly. We had three rooms booked for the night: 1, 17, and
20. With the six of us able to utilize equipment and three separate secluded areas to investigate, I felt it would be an eventful
night. Once the team arrived at the hotel, they took the opportunity to have dinner at the hotel since it was their last chance
for food until morning.

We returned to our room (room 17), and I took Ashley
around parts of the building to talk about the history and the
events that I had experienced there. We went into the poker
room and sat down. Through the window, we noticed that one
investigator and her roommate for the evening had returned to
their room from eating and wondered how they were going to

cope with each other for the entire night, given that they fought like brother and sister. Suddenly, the lights in the poker room started flickering on and off. We stepped away from the window and looked up, only to see the chandelier swinging back and forth. We looked around the room, taking note of anything out of the ordinary, and exited to the hallway and walked back to our room.

The other team was now organized, and we started the investigation. We walked down the hallway of the second floor and set up some EMF devices throughout. We sat down in the hallway, taking pictures and waiting for one of the devices to activate. Nothing happened. We moved into the poker room and sat at the table, asking questions and listening for noise, footsteps, and anything out of the ordinary. Again, nothing. Down at the bar, we tried communicating with various types of equipment with no success. During the course of the night, there were no occurrences that appeared strange or unusual. Ashley and I decided to go to bed. I felt it strangely unusual that I didn't even smell Mary's perfume in room 17. During previous visits, I smelled that perfume, but this time I did not. Overall, my final venture in the St. James was very quiet and uneventful.

Final Thoughts on the St. James Hotel

My final thoughts on the St. James Hotel are simply this: the hotel does have a paranormal environment wrapped around it, and at times you can experience things that are unexplainable and sometimes unbelievable. The one thing that I could not truly explain was the floral scent in room 17. I didn't matter what smell arose, whether it be a total bathroom blowout or the repulsive stench of a sauerkraut and barbeque sandwich,

the sweet, flowery smell would always come back with a ven-
geance. No air freshener. No hidden deodorizer. No explanation. I know it's not the most convincing evidence in the world.
I also know I don't have evidence backing up the experiences I
had with the bathroom apparition and other experiences. You
should go for yourself and have your own experiences. You will
not experience something paranormal every time you go, but
you are immersed in history and Western nostalgia.

I feel that the owners of the hotel should let investigators
into room 18. On several occasions we were told we couldn't
enter the room even for a picture. I know for a fact that investigators have been in there before, and I feel it would be beneficial to our research to have access to the room to document
the activity surrounding it. The first time I was at the hotel, the
investigator who accompanied me was talking through the door
to the entity and stated he felt a vibration in the floor next to
the door. I don't know if I necessary believe the legend of TJ
Wright, the TV reporter story, or even that TJ is the one haunting the room. I do believe, however, that there is a mystery held
inside the walls of room 18, and I hope that if the place sells to
a different owner or if the current owners change their mind,
we can gather much information about what is transpiring inside room 18.

The St. James Hotel has much to offer. Cimarron, New Mexico, is a beautiful and historic community with a peaceful and
relaxing atmosphere. There is not much to do or see in the town,
but it is a great place to go and relax for a couple of days to escape the insanity of big city life. The most amazing thing about
the St. James Hotel is the history behind it. Once you are inside
the hotel, you are taken back to the time of the Wild West. I can't
help but think that after all the deaths and gun fights, there is

emotional energy contained in some residual way in the hotel. So much energy, in fact, that there will be some remaining for the next hundred years.

So, if you do find yourself at the St. James Hotel, take notice late at night when the clock strikes twelve and the real show starts. The spiritual residents of the old saloon will be watching and waiting for the right opportunity to greet you firsthand.

Chapter 2
WAVERLY HILLS
SANATORIUM
Louisville, Kentucky

Perhaps one of the most famous haunted places in the United States is Waverly Hills Sanatorium. Anyone who has any interest in the paranormal has heard of Waverly Hills, and almost all of them have the desire to go there. Starting in 1908 as a two-story building and evolving into the extremely large and shut-down building it is today, Waverly Hills has seen its fair share of death and suffering. The sanatorium was closed in 1980 by the state and is today a museum and tour exhibition of the paranormal. The largest number of deaths at Waverly Hills took place during a tuberculosis outbreak in the early part of the twentieth century. It is estimated that thousands of people died in Waverly Hills as a result of the epidemic.

I do not know when the hauntings began in the building, but I can assure you that they continue today. Several television shows and books include details about Waverly Hills and the reported hauntings. If the thousands of people that died at Waverly were haunting the place, why stay? Could it be the

attention and admiration from all the tour members and paranormal investigators? If people suffered and died in the sanatorium, could they be desperately trying to escape the hell that
surrounds them?

I felt these were legitimate questions and I had ample opportunity to go and find answers. I know evidence can be falsified
and stories can be told, but I wanted solid proof for myself. I
wanted to have that personal experience and document it fully.
I was looking for the answers and would do almost anything to
have my chance to find them. Little did I know I was about to
get them.

Investigating Waverly Hills:
The Living, the Dead, and the Death Tunnel

I made a reservation for July 6, 2008. This investigation would
feature me; Tony, an investigator; Ashley; the mysterious investigator Meagan; the experienced and innovative investigator
Deanna; and the talented Michelle (who was the most beautiful
investigator I had met at the time). We found the front gate
with no problem. I could easily see the top of the building from
down the drive. The problem was that we could not see anyone
coming to let us in. I called the number listed on the sign to let
them know that we had arrived. No answer. Two investigators
exited the car to unlock the gate themselves and let us in.

As the gate was swinging open, I could see a golf cart in the
distance with two men heading our direction. *Damn,* I thought. I
knew we were about to get a quick lecture about passing the gate
with No Trespassing signs. When the cart pulled up, I quickly
announced that we had a reservation for the evening and was
educated about how opening the gate could lead to trouble. We
made the drive up to the building to wait for Tony and Deanna

to arrive so we could start the investigation. I got out the video camera and took a few outside shots of the building.

After a few phone calls and mixed directions from the locals, Tony and Deanna arrived. We gathered all the equipment and made our way into the main area, where the gift shop is located, to prepare for the investigation.

Our tour guide, Mike, asked if we wanted him to take us on a tour of the building. We all agreed, and I asked if it would be okay if I filmed the tour. He said yes, and we headed out. We started our tour at the death tunnel, or "body chute" as they called it. He explained about the actual use of the tunnel and how they used it to transport bodies when the death toll was at its peak. I had always had an interest in the death tunnel but didn't want to spend a lot of time there to investigate. Mike told us that approximately 63,000 people lost their lives in the building, most as a result of the tuberculosis outbreak.

We proceeded through each floor of the main hospital, hearing the stories associated with each one. I was familiar with the nurse who hung herself outside of room 502 on the fifth floor but I was unaware of the remaining stories. Mike told the story of a group of kids who broke into the hospital late one night and were trapped on the fourth floor by an unseen force. They used a hatchet to try and hack through the metal door in order to escape. They made it out of the building okay, but the evidence of the hatchet was still left in the door to this day. Mike also told us about the story of the homeless man and his dog who were thrown down one of the elevators on the third floor in a cult-related killing. This was said to have been documented as a homicide with the local police department.

One of the sanatorium's spirits was that of a child named Timmy who frequented the second floor. I once asked the owner if the name *Timmy* was accurate, and she said that it was a name picked up by a psychic who visited the building. While the name could not be validated, the activity that was created by the child could very well be. The child was said to roll balls down the hallway in a playful manner. The other areas with activity, unrelated to any particular story, were room 503, the morgue, the electroshock therapy room, the gift shop, the cafeteria and kitchen, and the occupational therapy room.

The First Floor

We started our investigation on the first floor and made our way through the entire hallway to the other side of the building, which had the staircase to the upper floors. As we explored the floor, we made basic observations of the areas and looked for a good place to conduct the first sit-down. We chose the occupational therapy room as our first sit-down area. As we settled in a space to sit and conduct the experiment, Tony took the EMF arrays (EMF meters that are soundless with LED lights to indicate activations) down the two hallways and set them up in a V-shaped pattern (to maintain visibility) leading directly to the room we were in. The thought of watching the arrays go off heading in our direction seemed like an appealing idea to me. We took our seats and, in the midst of the darkness, started the session.

We started by asking questions to see if we could solicit a response: "Who are you, and why are you here?" While we did not observe any array activations, we did hear several noises and bangs from the distance. I had to wonder with the bats and open windows if they could have been false positive noises. At one point I heard what I could only explain as a strange ringing sound, almost like a dial tone. The sound was distant and very faint, but it reoccurred three times in all. We concluded the sit-down in the occupational therapy room and proceeded to the modern-day gift shop.

We did some rearranging of the equipment and brought some of the EMF arrays into the room with us. Most of us stayed in the room; Tony was outside in the hallway and one investigator stood in the doorway. Again, we started with the questions. Deanna noticed that one of the arrays flickered or the light pattern changed. Immediately focusing my attention on her and the array, I asked her about the activation.

"I can't say for sure, but I saw the light increase from the meter," she said.

The only two possible ways for the light to increase on the array are an activation (picking up a field) or if the battery power is depleted. When the battery from the array is low, the green LED pilot light on the meter will be dim. When the power is low and the meter is activated, all the lights on the array will light up all at once and stay lit until the battery is changed or the power is turned off. Even if low battery were the issue, there would still have to be activation from the meter to make the light pattern occur. Either way, I found the occur-rence rather interesting, so I decided to keep an eye on that back wall.

We heard a few more noises from a distance but could not verify their origin or location. Ashley expressed feelings of ap-prehension in the building at this point and was a bit uncom-fortable. We decided to divide up and cover two more rooms before proceeding to the next floor.

We split into two groups and covered the electroshock ther-apy room and another down the hall. I sat in the electroshock room with Ashley and Michelle, and we spoke briefly to the spirits as I stood in the doorway filming the room and the hall-way. We did hear several noises that were later proven to be false positives, caused by the other team. With nothing more happening, we decided to take a break for a few minutes.

The Death Tunnel

The break gave us some opportunity to check the time and de-velop an efficient game plan for the rest of the building. The investigation of the death tunnel would be an appropriate ac-tion so that we could get it out of the way and not have to leave the building after that. We packed the gear up and headed to the dreaded body chute. Upon entrance of the tunnel, I set the camera up on the tripod before we made our way down. The tunnel was 485 feet down at a 45-degree angle. This was not going to be pleasant.

The women only went down about a quarter of the way, while Tony and I went down even farther. After passing the halfway point, I started getting very dizzy. I stopped and sat down. I told Tony that I had to wait for a few minutes to catch my balance. I felt like the entire room was leaning forward even though there was no movement. In addition to the dizziness, I felt like I was having trouble breathing. As I sat in the dark-ness, I looked up to see the faint light at the top of the tunnel when I started hearing a flapping sound. I shined my lights up and around and noticed a form coming down toward us. We ducked, avoiding a dive-bombing group of bats.

We stayed in the area a while longer, asking a few questions aloud and giving appropriate time for a response. The tunnel for the most part was very quiet and calm. My feelings of dizzi-ness and difficulty breathing died down a little over the course of the last few minutes we were in there. Tony and I made the long walk up the tunnel to the others and eventually the exit. We then walked back to the gift shop area for another break.

At this point it was obvious to me that we had a serious problem. We had only covered the first floor and death tunnel and it was already eleven thirty. We were almost at the halfway point of our investigation timeline. After a thorough discussion, we felt it would be easier to once again divide the group into two teams of three, with each group investigating one floor. Ashley, Michelle, and I started on the second floor. Tony, Deanna, and Meagan started on the fourth.

The Second Floor

As we began the walk-through of the second floor, I thought back to the tour and some of the things that the tour guide had mentioned to us to look for on this particular floor. I remembered hearing of the child known only as Timmy and the ball activity. Mike had also recommended to check out the kitchen and cafeteria. During our walk-through, we made several obvious attempts to communicate with a child. We took the toy ball that was already on the floor and used it in various experiments. We told the spirits that they could at any time make the ball roll down the hallway and we would gladly roll it back and play with them. At one point, it appeared that the ball was going to move, but it only shifted back and forth very faintly.

We went to the other side of the building and into the kitchen area for a while. Rather than performing a sit-down, we stood in the room and asked a few quick questions to see if one was warranted. Again, observing no activity, we felt it would be more beneficial to move on and find another location. We went to the cafeteria door on the other side of the hallway, but it was locked. We turned around and started down the hallway back to the other side when we heard footsteps coming from down the hallway.

"Hello?" we asked. No answer. We thought it was team two shifting or coming down the hallway. We still heard no response, but a figure appeared to be coming toward us from down the hallway.

A voice finally called out, "It's me."

It was Mike, our tour guide. He apologized for the door being locked and opened it up for us. I guess he could see us from the cameras around the hospital. We proceeded inside and prepared to perform a sit-down in the room. Before we could begin, I noticed that I needed another tape for record-ing. I didn't have one so I was going to have to go back down to the main area, where the rest of our equipment was. This was going to require me to go back down to the first floor ... alone.

I made my way to the first floor. I occasionally looked into the empty rooms with my flashlight and stopped every now and then to see if something would happen or if something would try and get my attention. I had no incident on the way to the gift shop. I grabbed a new tape and a drink of soda before heading back to the group. On my way back, I made a stop in the occupational therapy room for a few seconds to see if some-thing would happen. I thought I saw something coming toward my direction from the down the hallway. It was moving very slowly, almost as if it were crippled, with a limp or hobble. I didn't want to wait up for it to see what it was or what it wanted. I had no equipment and no way of documenting whatever was about to happen, so I walked straight to the stairwell and back up to the second floor.

I entered the cafeteria room and loaded the camera with a fresh tape. Once again, I set the camera up on the tripod and took a seat next to the other two investigators for the duration of the sit-down. We could faintly see inside the room from the light projected from the array.

We began asking if anyone was in the room and, if they were, if could they make a noise or give us indication that they were there. The room was fairly large and could have easily been called two separate rooms put together. It was as if someone had knocked down a wall dividing the rooms. They were very open with little to no equipment in them. The back of the large room was surrounded by darkness and had one single array in the center of it. I started asking direct questions about the room and its purpose during the hospital's days of functioning. I could see something in back corner of the room but could not tell what it was or what it was doing. It was moving and had no specific shape or form. I almost thought it was the same thing I saw on my way back from the gift shop area, only that one had a humanlike form. The quick, shadowlike form began to zoom inside the room: it moved so fast it was like the form was tele-porting from one area to the other instantaneously.

"Is there anyone in the room?" No response.

The anticipation of array activations or a noise had me a little uneasy.

"If there is anyone in the room, please do something," I stressed. We heard a knocking noise from the far corner of the room. The room was very still and quiet for a few minutes, so I felt was good time to get some EVP. Ashley took over asking ques-tions, which allowed me to put all my focus into the other side of the room. I can't tell you that being in the other side of the room was easy. I constantly felt like there was someone behind me, and I ended up standing with my back against the wall for the remain-der of our time in the room. After the questioning, we packed up to meet up with the other team in the stairwell and switched floors.

The Fourth Floor

We spoke briefly to the other team about their experiences on the fourth floor and then headed up there. We didn't know what to expect on the fourth floor since Mike had mentioned that this was one of the best floors in the building. It appeared to be darker than the previous ones.

We made our way down to the other side of the building and entered the operating room that Mike had told us on the tour that people kept getting trapped in. Apparently, the door would slam and they would not be able to get out. I set up the equipment and then took a seat on the floor. The room itself was fairly small compared to the other rooms, which I thought was strange, seeing that a room for medical operation would need more space. Meagan stayed in the hallway right outside in the event we did get trapped in. This would be the place to see if I could get the spirits to slam the door on command or at their own will. However, I did feel that this action was an end result of a mischievous temperament and didn't think they would slam the door on command, since to them it was better to frustrate or frighten the unsuspecting victim.

As I felt it was worth the chance, I asked if they could shut the door. The door did not budge. I even offered the perpetrator a bribe of screaming for my life if they would slam it. Again, the door did not move. I asked Meagan to pay specific attention to the hallway due to the feeling that if someone were out there, she might be able to get a visual on them. We had a few arrays outside the room and one inside the room. We heard a few distant noises from down the hall but again could not validate that they were something paranormal. After fifteen to twenty minutes in the room, we decided to make our way back to the other side of the building through the atrium, which is open to the outside. There was no glass in the windows along the atrium, and there was a lot of outside noise contamination. Tony had mentioned to us earlier that when they had investigated that part of the building, he had witnessed what appeared to be twinkling lights at the end of the section. We walked all the way through and did not encounter anything unusual.

The Morgue

By the time we reached the end of the hallway, it was time to meet back up with team two. We met them in the stairwell and decided to head back to the main area for another break. After the break, we reconfigured our schedule. It was almost two o'clock and we had a little over two hours left in the building with two whole floors to go. We decided to stay together as one whole group instead of breaking up. I wanted to go to the morgue area on the first floor before we went upstairs. I remembered watching the television show in which the teenage girls were in the morgue and the body table slid out from the cabinet. I decided to take the team into this room for a quick sit-down session.

As we entered the room, we noticed a body cabinet used to store bodies that would fit three. The room was fairly open itself and did not feel cramped. There was what appeared to be an embalming table next to the cabinet. Ashley decided that she wanted to climb into the cabinet and lie on the morgue slab tray. The middle tray seemed the sturdiest. We radioed the main office to be sure that there was not going to be a problem, and once we got the okay, she climbed in. I couldn't believe she was going to be able to stay inside that cabinet since she was previously so claustrophobic. She described the feeling in the cabinet as void of any feelings or sensations. She said it was very quiet and all the strange feelings that were in the room seemed to disappear when she entered the cabinet. She climbed out and we continued.

Soon after, Deanna started feeling ill. She said she felt like she was having a panic attack. Her heart rate increased and she was very uncomfortable. I asked her a few questions about her condition to see if it was asthma related or something else. I also asked if she wanted to go on with investigating or if she would like to go outside for a while. She said although it was an uncomfortable feeling, she wanted to continue the experience. Ashley suggested she lean into the cabinet and see if the feeling went away. She briefly stuck her head into the opening for a minute or two and said there was no effect. We all stayed in the room for several minutes and then proceeded up to the third floor.

The Third Floor

Once we entered the third floor, we conducted the first sit-down at the elevator shaft that a vagrant man and his dog were thrown down. Mike also suggested that we pay attention to the L-shaped linen closet behind the elevator. I positioned my camcorder into the room of the closet, and we took our position out in the hallway. Some of the investigators almost immediately identified a whistling noise. The noise seemed to have come from down the hallway opposite of where we were, in one room where none of us had been yet. We started asking questions and tried to get some communication going. I quickly observed shadowy movement down the hallway where the whistling originated. The shadow was very low to the ground and lasted only a few seconds before dissipating. I asked for a confirmation noise if someone was in the room with us. Silence.

After several minutes, Meagan decided to send a penny flying down the hallway in hopes of a response. I was concerned about making a bad impression on the long-departed guests of the hospital. During the time the hospital was active as a tuberculosis clinic, financial hardships were common, and I didn't want them to think we were making fun of them. I mean, if you were starving and some jerk threw a can of biscuits down the hall at you, you'd be pissed, right? I made it known to the spirits that we meant no disrespect and would like a response or sound.

The penny made its long journey down the long dark hallway only to bounce off the ground and land in an undetermined location. We waited to see if a response was coming. After minutes of silence, I tried a knock test.

"I'm going to knock a few times to let you know where I am, and if you could be so kind as to make a noise or do something to let us know where you are, I would greatly appreciate it," I stated loudly. I made three loud knocks that echoed in the halls of the sanatorium. Again, we got no response.

We then decided to head down the hallway to the other side of the building. At the hallway's end, I set up the camcorder on the tripod, and we all took a seat and started yet another session. After a few minutes of asking questions, I looked down the hallway through which we came and saw another shadow moving along the ground. No more than six inches high, it was very long in shape and almost appeared like it was slithering along the ground about forty feet down the hall from us.

At almost the same time, a few team members heard an audible giggle or voice from the room. I did not hear the voice myself but believed that something was going on inside the room. I started asking questions to see if someone was trying to get our attention.

"Could you make more noises or come closer in the room we're standing in?" The room was once again quiet.

Deanna decided at that point to try another experiment. She had a ball that she wanted to roll down the dark hallway to see if whatever was there would roll it back to us in hopes of further communication. She announced herself and then rolled the ball down the hallway. The room was quiet. I looked around the dark hallway to see if I could pinpoint something moving or shifting. I could not see or feel any proof of environmental or physical changes, and the equipment did not register anything.

Then we heard noises from the back corner of the room. Several isolated noises had manifested in that area of the room earlier, but these were getting louder. I made the comment that whatever was in the room had something to do with the far back corner. As soon as I made that comment, there were no more noises. It was like once I identified where they were or where had been, they made no effort to do anything else.

The rest of the sit-down on that floor was quiet and uneventful. The time was 2:55 a.m., and we had little over an hour to complete the last area of the building, the area I was the most eager to get to: the fifth floor. We made the climb up two floors to the top of Waverly Hills Sanatorium. The one and only thing that I had heard about the floor was the story of room 502, outside of which a nurse was found hanging. I felt it was going to be an interesting final hour.

The Fifth Floor

We arrived on the fifth floor and started setting up in the middle of the hallway. This floor comprised a hallway as well as a few small rooms, such as 502 and 503. On each side of the hallway were two large rooms that gave access to the roof from each one. The first things that I wanted to pay close attention to were room 502 and the outside area. I set up my camcorder to record the inside of room 503 for the remainder of the evening. I also set an EMF array on a small chair in the room as well. We took a seat in the hallway, and I sat next to the doorway of 502.

Almost immediately, Deanna spotted a shadow in the corner of one of the rooms. She said it went away quickly, but I knew that this was a sign that we were not alone. She started asking the dark figure questions and tried to coax it to reappear. After several failed attempts, she decided to try and roll another ball. She made the announcement and rolled the ball to Ashley, who then rolled the ball out to the middle of the room.

"Will someone roll it back to me or another person?" she asked. The room was very still for the next minute or two, and the ball failed to move. "If you change your mind, you can roll it anytime you wish."

I wanted to focus on the nurse who hung herself outside room 502.

"If the nurse is there, can she please make a noise to alert us of her presence?" I asked. A noise came from room 502. I asked for another knock for validation of her presence, and two noises again came from the room. I thanked her for the effort and began asking her direct questions. I made the mistake of asking her why she wanted to end her life, and it caused a dramatic environmental change. A frigid cold air blasted through the area I was in, and I got the distinct feeling of apprehension and shame mixed with a little anger. I knew that I would be outside on the roof in a little while and didn't want an angry spirit pushing me over. In light of that, I didn't feel it was appropriate to continue asking questions, so we let the quiet take the room over before we headed to another room.

The two rooms that gave access to the roof were our two final destinations on the floor. We started in the one to the left of 502. We entered the room and scattered. As everyone settled, we continued asking questions. I asked if someone there was looking for their family, but I could not get any response and kept getting pulled back into the previous hallway. I asked aloud if someone there would like us to reenter the hallway and heard no response. The time kept slipping away, and we knew we had another room to check out.

Upon entering the final room, I thought it would be a good idea to try the ball experiment myself. I picked up a small round ball that fit in the palm of my hand and started talking. I stated my intentions: "I will bounce the ball in the hallway, and, if you can, would someone bounce it back or toss it to another location?" I bounced the ball into the darkness and listened to the bouncing across the floor. No response was given.

In a last effort, Ashley and Deanna came up with a plan: they decided to play a game and see if it would spawn a reaction. They got up and stood in the middle of the floor. Then they started moving in a circle, singing "Ring around the Rosy," and fell to the ground. They asked if anyone would like to join in on the fun and games. They even invited them to play games of their own. It was a really big place to play hide and seek, but we were too short on time to get involved in such a game.

Before long, we heard several footsteps in the stairwell and a flashlight shining from below. Mike had come through the door. We asked if our time was up, and he said we had about five minutes left. We used the last five for discussion of what had happened throughout the night and some of the impressions we had of the building. At the four o'clock mark, we made the long descent to the main area to pack up and go home. It seemed like the night flew by, but we were all tired and exhausted from the investigation and welcomed a good night's sleep.

Final Thoughts on Waverly Hills Sanatorium

Even though we did not collect a lot of physical evidence, it was still very much worth the trip and the money to investigate Waverly Hills Sanatorium. Several things happened to us that we cannot pass off as coincidence, and we did capture a few EVP and photo anomalies. Several of us had personal experiences, but we cannot conclude they were paranormal due to the lack of evidence.

The staff was excellent and accommodated us at their every chance. Overall, I would say that it was one of the more memorable investigations I have had in a while. I can't say for sure why Waverly Hills could very well be haunted. I know the deaths from the tuberculosis outbreaks could have a big part, but there were other feelings present there besides suffering and death. I believe that some of the departed souls from family members could have returned to the building to seek out relatives and friends who were treated there.

I believe the building hosts significant activity at times, but as I know from investigating buildings in the past, the activity level varies from time to time. I don't know who or how many people are still lurking behind the walls at Waverly Hills, but I know some of them are willing to communicate with you under the right circumstances. I highly recommend taking the chance and investigating Waverly Hills for the possibility of having the spirits of the dead walk the halls in attempt to welcome you to the place they call home.

Chapter 3

THE VILLISCA
AX MURDER HOUSE

Villisca, Iowa

If you would have said the words *Villisca Ax Murder House* nine or ten years ago, hardly anyone would have known what you were talking about. Today, however, it has become known as one of the most haunted houses in America. This house is one you will find tucked away in the small community of Villisca, Iowa. The small two-story house is located on the edge of a normal, everyday neighborhood. Before I get into all the exciting events in this chapter, let me first tell you about the tragic events that led to the haunting of the house.

The year was 1912. Josiah B. Moore and his family lived in the house very happily until the tragic night of June 10. On that fateful night, someone entered the home of the Moore family with an ax and murdered Josiah, his wife Sarah, their four children (Herman, Katherine, Boyd, and Paul), and two children (Lena and Ina Stillinger) who were guests sleeping in the first-floor bedroom. What makes this story even more tragic is the fact that even with numerous suspects and hours of extensive investigations, the murder was never solved and no one was ever charged with the crime.

The Villisca Ax Murder House.

In 1994 the house was purchased by Darwin and Martha Linn. They turned the house into a museum and now lease it out overnight to paranormal investigators much like myself for the purpose of documenting the activity within. I originally learned of the house through an internet broadcast of a local Iowa newscast. The house intrigued me, but, according to the news broadcast, it was nearly impossible to get into due to it being booked six months in advance. It wasn't until 2007 that I would get the chance to drive to Villisca and have my first set of experiences in the very much haunted home of the Moore family.

First Investigation: The Face in the Window

On April 28, 2007, we started preparing to drive to Villisca. On this particular trip would be Ashley, Tony, Meagan, and I.

Tony had traveled to Oklahoma several days earlier to visit with relatives who lived in the city. I talked with him briefly and we headed north to our destination.

We arrived in the town shortly before sundown. While the town was very small, we felt it was hard to navigate where we were going. We stopped in the grocery store to try to get directions to Darwin's Villisca museum. After a few U-turns, we pulled up to the museum and walked inside. We met with Darwin, who asked if he could give us a tour of the town before we headed to the house. We had no objection and agreed to follow him to the various locations he wanted to show us. We followed him around town as he pointed out the homes of the key players during the time of the murder. We ended up at the local cemetery, where the Moore family and Stillinger girls were buried, and then headed to the house.

As we pulled up to the house, an eerie feeling came over me. The daylight started to dim away, and the darkness of night was setting in. I looked at the house and got the impression of several people looking out the window anxious to greet us. We exited the car and made our way to the barn next to the house. The barn was the area where we would have power, plumbing, and refrigeration for the evening. We decided to make this place our meeting point or "base camp" for breaks and planning. We signed the rental agreement contact supplied by Darwin, and I paid him the rest of the money owed for the night's investigation.

I took a few minutes to go through my equipment and looked up only to notice that a car had arrived. There was a small group of teenagers standing in the yard in front of the house. I didn't think much about it until one investigator came into the barn and said we had a problem. Apparently, the kids had come up out of curiosity to see what we were doing, and one of them started singing. When asked why she was singing, the girl replied that it keeps the demons away because they don't like her to sing to God. I felt this could be an issue if it continued throughout the night or if the kids came back later on. I talked briefly with one of them, who said that if I wanted him to, he would come back and show me some evidence he had gotten out of the home. He gave me a contact phone number, and they got in their car and left. We continued into the house with Darwin.

Once we were all inside, I followed Darwin to each room as he lit several lanterns. We were on the top floor of the house when he opened the door to the attic area and headed inside.

"Come in," a voice whispered.

Startled, I asked Darwin if someone was already in the room, but he said no and continued. I looked around, halfway expecting another investigator to be inside trying to scare us. No one was there. I told Darwin what I had heard as we walked into the room, but he didn't pay any mind to it. He exited the attic and started back down the stairs. We ended up in the living room of the house, where Darwin finished the story of the murders and proceeded to "communicate with the spirits." He used a pendulum and started asking questions to Sarah Moore. He appeared to have some positive answers in accordance to the movement of the pendulum. After the session, he asked if we needed anything else and left for the evening.

As always, we found a local convenience store for energy drinks, snacks, and other necessities. During our trip down the street, we met up again with Darwin at the store. I purchased about twenty dollars' worth of food and proceeded outside to talk to Darwin. We thanked him again and made our way back up the street to the home.

Once back at the house, we unloaded the food into the refrigerator and started getting equipment together. I decided to run my video camera and have Tony document the environmental readings. Ashley had her camera, and Meagan had an EMF detector. Audio would also be captured during this investigation, one of the more promising pieces of evidence we would get due to the history of EVP gathered at the house from other investigators. One thing I felt was odd was the fact that most of the EVP captured was a female child. There were three female children killed in the home, and I wanted to make a connection with her so that I could see which one was trying to talk to everyone.

We started our sweep in the living room of the house. As we made our way through, I began to pay attention to each room. I felt something in three rooms: the main floor guest room, the upstairs parents' room, and the living room.

First was the guest room. This was the room where Lena and Ina Stillinger took their last breaths. Nothing much was in this room but a dresser, a bed, and blue walls. There was a window that oversaw the back of the house. When I entered the small blue room, I immediately paused. I felt several things. There was a feeling of unease coming from right behind me. It was if I could feel someone standing right behind me, which was bizarre since I was almost against the wall. With the history of the room, I concluded it could have been the presence of either. I also felt that this would be one of the places we would have a higher success rate at capturing phenomena or communicating with a spirit in the home. I left a digital recorder on the dresser for EVP.

After five minutes or so, we moved on to the upstairs part of the home. The staircase itself had an interesting feeling to it. Several of us commented that it felt like someone was following you up or down. It felt like the presence was right on your shoulders. We reached the second floor of the house, which is divided into three areas: the parents' room, the kids' room, and the attic room.

The first room by the stairs was the parents' room. Upon entering the room, I felt compelled to sit on the bed. There were several items of antiquity around the room. I don't know if these items were genuine and belonged to the Moore family or not. There was one bed and a small dresser by a window with white drapes. The room connected to both the attic room and the kid's bedroom. I sat on the edge of the bed and remained quiet for a minute. A shaking sensation came over me, as if the bed were shaking very violently, yet the bed never moved. The bizarre vibration feeling only lasted a few seconds.

I felt that this room was the point of entry for something very sinister and dark. Not a demon but rather a spirit in the house that liked to torment not only the living guests in the house but the spirits in it as well. Yes, I believe the killer of the Moore family returned to the house and is very much one of the resident ghosts. I'll describe my experiences with that a little later.

We continued our sweep to the kids' room. This room was next to the parents' room. There were two small beds and a crib. A small closet also accompanied the room. This was another area of interest for investigators due to the closet door opening and closing on its own. We decided we would come back to the room throughout the night and experiment with the door.

The attic room was the final room on our list for the upstairs area. This was probably the creepiest of the rooms. Two *Amityville Horror*–style windows were the only light source. There were a few chairs in the room, and the floors were wood with several wood beams in the center of the room. We entered and searched the area. Many theorize that the killer hid out in this room, waiting for the Moore family to come home and go to bed before starting his executions. I didn't feel anything strange even though I heard the voice earlier in the night. I did, however, want to spend a little time in the room later in the night.

Once back downstairs, we went back into the living room. This was the most open room in the house. There was a couch that was very near the room where the Stillinger girls were killed. This room is another room that interested me because I felt it was a meeting point for the spirits in the house—I guess you could say "a place of gathering."

We took a quick break for snacks and drinks and decided to perform a sit-down session in the living room. We set out the EMF arrays in all areas of the living room and in the doorway of the guest room. I also set the Trifield natural meter, an EMF meter that is sensitive to motion as well as electromagnetic fields, on the dresser in the blue room. We each took a seat around the room and began the communication process.

"If there is anyone in the room, can you make yourself known?" we asked. "We want to know what happened here and who committed these horrible crimes."

Silence filled the room. We could hear nothing from either floor. We then started talking specifically to the Stillinger girls, asking if they could they make themselves known if they were present. We also asked if they could show us where they were.

The Trifield in the guest room started going off. It started activation in a very low tone and then started activating from low to high rapidly.

"If Lena or Ina is in the room playing with the 'blue box,' can you make a loud noise inside the room and let us know you're there?"

Suddenly, a few tapping sounds manifested inside the dark room. The sounds were repetitive and to me sounded like someone tapping the end of a pencil on the dresser.

"If someone is inside the room making the tapping sound, can you give us another definite sign of your presence?"

A few moments later I could see a light flash on the wall in the room. It didn't take me long to realize that one of the arrays positioned inside the room must have activated. I asked the group if any of them had witnessed the activation of the array. Tony was the only one that could have seen it since he was sitting across the doorway, but he said he didn't catch it.

A sudden shaking sound came from inside the room. It was very loud and quick, like someone had run into the dresser in the room. I stood up to walk into the room and see if anything that was on the dresser had moved or fallen to the floor. I shined my flashlight on the dresser and nothing seemed out of place. Even the equipment that was placed on top of the dresser had not been disturbed. I returned to the living room and sat back down in my chair. We continued our various communication techniques for about fifteen more minutes with no noises or responses. We concluded the sit-down and decided that we would take another break and perform our next sit-down in the upstairs kids' room.

After the break, we all gathered upstairs in the Moore children's room and took seats on the floor and on the bed. We focused the camera on the closet door, which was notorious for moving on its own and on command. We also set up the Trifield meter on the floor in the closet and EMF arrays around the kids' room and in the parent's room. We started the sitdown again, asking for anyone who could hear us to let us know by making a noise or activating one of the available meters. Even though we had various EMF arrays in the room, all eyes were on the closet door.

I then had a brilliant idea. Inside the barn was an old, worn ax that had been used over the years. It was not the original ax used in the murders, but it was scary-looking nonetheless.

"I'm going to bring the ax into the house to see if it sparks any activity," I said. Ashley and Meagan informed me that they would be getting the hell out of the house and that I could do as I pleased with the ax. They would not stay in the house if the ax were present and asked that I let them know when I was finished with whatever I was going to do. Tony agreed to stay.

I walked down the stairs and into the barn to grab the ax and then returned to the house. As I entered, I immediately felt another strange sensation. The only way I could describe it was that it was like the house took a deep breath when it saw me come in with the ax. I stood in the kitchen briefly and then walked up the staircase. As I passed the entryway from the kitchen, I heard a voice over my right shoulder say, "Thought so." The voice was so quick I could almost not understand what it was saying. I did not catch the voice on the digital recorder. I wanted to be sort of creepy with my appearance to spook Tony, since he was left alone in the upstairs bedroom of the house and would see a figure coming toward him dragging an ax. I hit the top of the floor and turned to face the doorway to the room Tony was in. I turned the blade of the ax to get the moonlight to reflect from it and slowly hobbled his way. Tony looked completely unmoved and unimpressed with my charade, so I entered the room and stood near the bed.

Again we started communication techniques. This time I used the ax as an area of focus. "If there is anyone in here, can you tell me if the ax being in the house makes you nervous?" I asked.

There was dead silence. Not like the silence of being alone in the room but rather the silence of people who don't want to say anything. I was hoping that I didn't create an image so frightful that the spirits in the house wouldn't communicate with me anymore. I then asked for the killer to become known. I thought about asking questions about the ax and started walking around the room swinging the ax along the way.

"Do I make you nervous, Mr. Killer?" I asked. An audible two-syllable word came from the other room. I couldn't tell if it originated in the attic area or Josiah and Sarah's bedroom, and the voice was mumbled. I could not make out what it was saying. Tony remained calm and assisted me in asking questions. We finished our session and both made our way downstairs. I looked back up briefly and got a quick glimpse of a black figure leaning over the stairs. I said nothing and made my way down the stairs.

Ashley and Meagan were sitting on the swing on the porch of the barn. After I returned the ax to its rightful place in the barn, we decided to try another sit-down in the living room. We again took a seat on the couch and started asking questions. This time Ashley had a few questions of her own.

She started talking to Sarah Moore. I had told her about the atmospheric change when I brought the ax in the house, and she felt Sarah was somehow involved. She started asking Sarah if she was uncomfortable with the ax being in the house. The air immediately got colder and somewhat of a draft manifested. (Again, my attention was focused on the guest room.) Ashley felt that Sarah was angry because the ax scared the children in the house, and perhaps they were all hiding in the guest room. The strange sensations persisted throughout her questioning.

Tony then took a different approach. He asked to speak with the parents of the children. He explained how he himself had children and would be devastated if anything ever happened to them. He showed empathy to the family wanting to protect their children and asked if they could do something to let us know they were in the house. A sudden popping noise came from inside the room. We could not conclude it was paranormal in nature but could not identify the source of the noise either. The session ended shortly after, and we returned to the barn.

While we were in the barn, we noticed several video tapes scattered inside the barn. One of the tapes was labeled something like "Scariest Places on Earth: Villisca, Iowa." After locating an extension cord that could reach from the barn to the living room, we moved the TV into the living room and prepared to watch the tape. It's a unique feeling to watch something about murders while you're sitting right inside the very house in which they took place.

As we watched the show, activity was brewing upstairs. When we went back upstairs after the show was over, the door to the attic had been moved slightly.

It was getting late, and we decided to attempt sleep inside the house. Tony agreed to brave the second floor all by himself. He took his sleeping bag and made his way upstairs. Meagan decided to sleep on the couch in the living room, and Ashley and I shared an inflatable mattress on the floor next to her. I was curious about how I was going to sleep with all the energy in the house. I didn't feel uncomfortable lying there trying to go to sleep, but I halfway expected to be awoken by some loud noise or scream. It wasn't until the next morning I found out that was far from true.

I awoke thinking I had a peaceful night's rest, and I had no recollection of what had happened from the time I went to sleep until the time I got up. All I could remember was waking up briefly and hearing the girls talking about Tony coming downstairs. I assumed that he had seen something or heard something that frightened him or that it was too uncomfortable to stay upstairs. I expected to see him on the floor of the living room or kitchen fast asleep in his sleeping bag.

Both women were frightened and shook up about something. They told me that two events had taken place over the course of the night. The first happened right after I went to sleep. I sat up on the mattress like I had awoken suddenly. My eyes were open, and I seemed to have a blank stare on my face. Ashley grabbed my arm and asked if I was okay, and I then stood up and faced the kitchen. She grabbed my ankle and asked again, but I walked toward the door as if I were going outside.

She commented that if I had gone outside, went into the barn, and came out with the ax, both of them were going to bar the door with something and escape from the back somehow. (Poor Tony would have been left to fend for himself.) I then returned to the living room and went back to sleep on the mattress.

A bit later in the morning, the second event occurred. Ashley and Meagan were both lying there talking when they heard footsteps coming down the staircase very slowly. They discussed that Tony must have been coming down the stairs, and

I assume this was the point when I woke up and heard them talking. The footsteps went to the base of the steps and started into the kitchen. Any moment they had expected to see Tony peer around the corner or step into the room, but he did not. The footsteps did not continue—something had walked into the room unnoticed and disappeared. We later learned that Tony did not even wake up at any point during the night, let alone come downstairs.

After very little sleep, we all got up and started getting ready for the day. We went down to the gas station and got something to eat, since it would be a while before any of us had a meal. When we returned, we did a quick inventory of the equipment and packed it all in the car. Ashley took pictures of the exterior of the house. I started up the stairs when I felt something pull on the sleeve of my shirt. I quickly turned around to find Tony coming through the doorway at the bottom of the stairs. I looked on the wall to see if my shirt could have gotten caught on a nail or sharp edge, but I could find nothing.

We went outside for a group photograph by the sign of the house. After making one last check, we got in the car and started back to Oklahoma. I couldn't help but feel like I was missing something. I knew that even with everything that happened, there was much more to be seen and experienced. We made a stop in Springfield, Missouri, dropped Tony off at his residence, and then headed back home.

A week or so later I was on the computer looking at the pictures that Ashley had taken, hoping to spot visual anomalies and such. I clicked each one to enlarge it and look for anomalies. Before I had looked at them, Tony told me to disregard the one with the head in the upstairs window because he was goofing off and didn't want me to mistake it for something paranormal. The photo he was talking about was the second of three photos taken in the same position, and two of them were missing a Tony head.

The first of the three had something different. In the bottom-floor window of the guest room there was what appeared to be a child's face was. I zoomed in on the face to see if I could make more details out of it. I did see what appeared to be facial features of a child. I checked the other two photographs to ensure the detail wasn't there—it was not. I then compared the facial features to those of the three girls who were killed in the house. The face was strikingly familiar to that of Ina Stillinger. Everything from the jawline to the barrette in her hair was identical. I was shocked, but the biggest contributing piece of evidence was yet to come.

Ashley and I were inside a clothing store in Northwest Oklahoma City when we received a phone call from Meagan. She sounded very excited and could not wait to tell us what she discovered. Apparently, she had captured the voice of a little girl on her audio recorder right outside of the room where the Stillinger girls were killed, though she could not make out what the child was saying. A day or so later Ashley and I met with Meagan to examine the EVP for ourselves. The voice was clearly that of a female child, but the words were almost scrambled. The only word we could all come to agreement on was *tonight*. Both pieces of evidence were compelling and conclusive, and another trip to Villisca, Iowa, was in order.

Second Investigation: When Ironing Boards Attack

The second trip to Villisca took place on June 17, 2007. A credit card error from the previous trip resulted in me being charged double, and I asked Darwin if he would put the money toward another night in the house instead of a refund. The night prior, Ashley, Deanna, Meagan, Tony, and I had investigated the Lemp Mansion in St. Louis, Missouri, and decided to head out from there. This time we had Deanna traveling with us for her first time at Villisca.

When we pulled up to the house, I knew there was something different about it this time. It looked very dark and empty. We got out of the car and walked inside the house. I didn't have the same initial feelings as I did last time of being watched and something waiting for us to start the investigation. The environment was different, as the weather was very hot and humid, but I didn't feel this had an impact on the activity of the house. I was thankful there was a window air-conditioning unit in the Moore children's bedroom. We unpacked the equipment and had a quick meeting in the barn. Everyone was assigned a task for the evening involving collecting evidence or recording data. After gathering the equipment, we started our baseline sweep of the house for readings.

We made our way through most of the house and documented no abnormalities until we reached the kitchen pantry. The pantry was small, so there was no way we could all fit in there. We took turns going inside and taking readings. A few of us had briefly stepped inside to get the EMF readings and temperature. Suddenly, an ironing board jumped off the pantry wall and flew at Deanna. We all gathered around the board and began taking photographs in hopes of capturing something. I checked on Deanna, who appeared to be shaken by the event. She said she was okay and ready to proceed with the investigation. Upon further examination, we noticed that the ironing board was hung on the wall by hooks, not nails. Whatever moved it would have had to lift the ironing board up before it threw it.

Next, we started the first sit-down in the blue room (the guest room or Stillinger room) due to the nature of the evidence we received on our last trip. With several meters placed in different areas of the room and multiple audio recorders running, we started asking questions to any spirits that may be present. At one point, Deanna heard something that compelled her to look down at the water bottle sitting on the floor next to her. It was then that she witnessed the bottle actually lift about an inch off the ground and fall to its side. We examined the bottle and tried to re-create the event by simply knocking the bottle over and then by lifting it and dropping it, but we could not get the bottle to land on its side and not roll forward. We continued the sit-down only to hear a few noises and taps before deciding to move on to another room.

We took a small break and moved into the living room. The noises continued, as it appeared we made contact with a spirit in the house through Meagan's dowsing rods. We could only get minimal information communicating. The basic questions (e.g., if someone is here, did they die here, etc.) are the only thing we could get the rods to cross, or acknowledge, a response for.

All of a sudden, Tony decided to try something. He had a ball he was playing with that he rolled into the blue room that rolled back to him and never bounced back against the wall. We were all amazed as to how this ball seemed to stop in the room and then roll itself back to us as if it were caught by a small child or intelligent spirit. This went on for about five minutes.

Despite all this activity going on, I did not yet feel any spirits in the house. We took another break and headed to the local convenience store.

Upon our return, we focused our investigation on the second floor of the house. Again, the closet door appeared to be the main interest. At this point my consciousness was hanging by a thread. We had EMF arrays and the Trifield meter set up in the children's room and the parents' room. We tried several times to get some meter activations from the spirits but had no success.

We did, however, get a positive response to a knock test. As we were all sitting in a circle in the kids' room, Tony said, "I'm going to knock on the floor three times, and would someone kindly knock back so we would have an idea where you are?" In response to his knocking, three faint knocks came from somewhere directly below us downstairs. The interesting thing is the room directly downstairs was the blue room, where the girls were murdered. We waited and listened for further noises or voices coming from downstairs, but they never came. We asked a few questions but again heard nothing.

After that we called it a night and went to sleep. Tony and Deanna decided to sleep on the main floor while the rest of us slept in the upstairs kids' room. There were no disturbances or occurrences during the night. The next morning, we awoke to once again take pictures and make our final rounds of the house. As we finished, I took one final walk around the barn. Having little experience or time in there, I decided to do a quick EVP session, which yielded no positive results. We packed up the car and started the long journey home.

Upon the review of our evidence, we found that we didn't capture any EVP or visual anomalies in the photographs. Personal experiences were the only evidence we had but were, however, documented on video.

Third Investigation:
There's Something under the Bed

My final trip to the notorious paranormal hot spot took place in the spring of 2010. I was traveling with Betty (a supposed psychic), Justin (aka Sweetness), Roy (a fellow investigator) and my best friend Cathy (an investigator and photographer). It was totally dark when we arrived at the house, so we unloaded our cases and took a quick tour. We set up the digital video recording system, which consisted of four cameras in separate rooms.

Roy was feeling ill but decided to come with me upstairs. We went into the Moore children's bedroom and started looking around. We already had a camera set up in the room but were trying to find a good spot for other equipment. Roy noticed that the sheet or blanket was hanging off the bed and went to tuck it in. When he lifted the blanket, a blue toy ball shot out from under the bed. He let out a shriek of sheer terror as he flung himself back to distance himself from the bed. I too was startled, and it appeared both of us had a different reaction to the situation: Roy thought the ball was a rat and was moving away from it; I thought there was actually someone under the bed who had broken into the house and could be potentially waiting to add more victims to the house's murderous history. As we both assured ourselves that neither was the situation, we headed back to the main floor to the rest of the team.

Back downstairs, Cathy was having problems locating some of her equipment, which we later determined was left behind in Oklahoma. We then started our investigation of the house. I was pleased to learn that many of the feelings I experienced on the previous visits were not only still present but also felt by the other investigators. Roy stayed downstairs and watched the DVR monitors while the rest of us went upstairs to attempt to document activity.

We spent the night taking readings and asking questions. Betty picked up on some of the family members in the house. There was no notable activity throughout the night. Then, at long last, we decided to try to get some sleep. Everyone decided to sleep upstairs in the children's room … everyone except me. I chose to sleep in the Stillinger girls' room completely alone on the first floor. As I lay there in the bed that may or may not have been the bed on the day of the murders, I stared up at the ceiling, wondering what was going to happen throughout the night. This was also the room where the ax that the murderer used in the killings was left.

Suddenly, a loud and frightening scream echoed through the house from the second floor. There was a loud crash, and the ceiling moved as if something fell from the second floor. I then realized that it was the scream of Roy, who was with me earlier in the evening.

"Is everything okay up there?" I asked. They called back that it was, and we went to sleep.

The next day, I asked what the screaming was all about. Roy had stated that he was sleeping on the floor next to one of the beds. As he lay awake, he turned over on his side, which positioned him looking directly under the bed. Out of the darkness came a small child moving toward him. He screamed and jumped back, which explained what I had heard. Once he looked back under the bed, the child was gone. He stated that the event happened so fast he was unable to offer a physical description of the child, but it seemed to be female and between six and eight years old. This would fit the profile of one of the

Stillinger girls; however, we cannot say which one or explain why she would be in the upstairs bedroom under the bed.

When we reviewed our evidence, we found that we had captured quite a few EVP. One of the most impressive to me was the one that was captured when we were setting up the equipment. Justin brought in a large case from outside and he was asking where we wanted him to put it. A voice came in after and said, "Don't ... put ... that ... there." The voice was very low but very clear. I felt the investigation was a success overall and will return in the future.

Final Thoughts on the Villisca Ax Murder House

Many of you might have a few questions about the Villisca Ax Murder House. First and foremost, is the Villisca Ax Murder House haunted? In my opinion, very much so. There are hundreds of people's experiences and hours of evidence to support that claim.

Not only is it haunted, but it's haunted in a unique way. There are voices, sounds, movements, and other pieces of evidence, but the house also presents certain vibes. I had the feelings of being watched and that someone was following me around the house when I was alone, just to name a few. Were those feelings caused by the actual spirits of the Stillinger girls or the murderer of the Moore family still in the house? I can't say for sure, but we do have evidence to support that there is possibly a residual haunting of the murders or the people involved. I didn't individually pick up on or communicate with any of the Moore family, although some other team members did.

The murderer's presence (or energy) is very menacing, overbearing, and ominous in the home. I felt a heavy negative feeling at times that may or may not be a direct result of the murders. As far as the killer goes, I think the spirit wants to make you uncomfortable while you are in the house. It has a taunting manner to it and believes it can get away with making you feel intimidated. Of the two main spiritual energies in the home, this is the strongest; however, it is not the most noticeable. I believe the second spirit that dominates the house is the spirit of a Stillinger girl. We can't say which one for sure, but in my opinion and based on the evidence we collected, it's Ina Stillinger. The facial features of the pictures and the voice on the recorder indicate a young child. Other investigations mostly pick up on Lena, so if we were to weigh the statistics, she is more likely the one we picked up on.

I feel the Stillinger spirit exhibits many different emotions at different times. I got a playful, innocent feeling at times and a scared, threatened feeling at others. I felt at times like I was shielding her from someone wanting to cause her harm, much like my experience in the blue room the first time I went to the house. I also could sense the feeling of being lost. Many times I feel that spirits of children cannot understand the concept of death. Some of them search for their parents and for some love and attention.

I also feel that our personal energies conflict with the energy of spirits. I don't know if they can necessarily read our energies or if they just attracts them. This was a similar experience I had with the spirit of a young girl at the Stone Lion Inn in Guthrie, Oklahoma (see chapter 7). Nevertheless, we had no problem establishing the communication with the spirits of the home.

Will I be returning to Villisca? Most definitely. I would love to examine the house once again with a team and draw our own conclusions about what happened on that violent night in 1912. Sadly, Darwin passed away a few years back, so if you are interested in your own investigation of the home, please contact

Martha Linn on the official Villisca Ax Murder House website. I feel the spirits of Stillinger girls are a welcoming and playful presence in the home; however, there still remain other spirits that I feel are unknown in the house as well. I'm not sure of the origin of these spirits, but I do know at the right moment they will appear from beyond the shadows of darkness at night and play with you too.

Chapter 4
THE MYRTLES PLANTATION
St. Francisville, Louisiana

The Myrtles Plantation has been recognized as both historical and haunted. But what is it exactly that makes it so haunted? Well, the history may hold a key to the answer.

The Myrtles Plantation has been around for over two hundred years and is said to be one of the most haunted houses in the United States. Built in 1787 by General David Bradford, the Myrtles Plantation has seen its fair share of tragic events. It is rumored that several people have been killed on the property.

One of the most famous of the stories is that of Chloe, a house servant to Judge Clark Woodruff. Chloe was rumored to be the mistress of the judge and would often eavesdrop on his conversations. At one point, the judge had enough of Chloe's spying and had her left earlobe cut off. She was then ordered to work in the kitchen. Chloe had a plan to get back into the family's good graces. Before this could happen, she had to gain the trust of the judge back. Her plan was to make the family sick; she would care for them until they regained their health, and they would welcome her back into the house. She made a

birthday cake for one of the children, adding poisonous olean-
der leaves to the recipe.

Her plan didn't go as she had hoped: even after an antidote,
the poison was too strong and killed the judge's wife and two
children. Shortly after her trial, Chloe was said to have been
hung and thrown into the river. She is one of the more famous
resident ghosts at the Myrtles and has even appeared in some
photographs taken at the plantation.

Investigating the Myrtles Plantation:
A Birthday to Remember

I had been intrigued by the Myrtles since I was young and had
always wanted to go there to investigate for the spirits that are
said to haunt the home and the surrounding grounds. I made
reservations at the Myrtles for Ashley and me for two nights.
I didn't think I would be spending my first night ever at the
Myrtles on my birthday, but that ended up being the case. We
arrived in St. Francisville shortly after five thirty in the evening
on February 8, 2007, the day of my twenty-eighth birthday.

Pulling up to the Myrtles, I had felt a small rush of adrena-
line run through me. I couldn't believe that I was actually here.
We pulled up to the property and parked the car. After picking
up the keys as well as a few informative papers, we finally made
our way into the house and up to our room for the first night.

I booked two separate rooms for the two nights we would
be staying there. The first night we stayed in the Ruffin Ster-
ling Room. This was a second-floor room with one queen-size
bed and a few chairs within it. The style of the room was very
antique-looking with a brilliant chandelier and decor throughout the room. I chose this room because it was the former
children's room, and I had heard stories about the children

causing disturbances in the middle of the night. It would be a great chance to set up equipment for documentation of this. We moved all equipment and luggage into the room and set up the arrays in the main hallway and staircase. We were fortunate enough to have that side of the house to ourselves. We sat in the hallway with the lights out and arrays active. I placed an audio recorder on the cabinet sitting in the hallway. I proceeded to conduct communication experiments as normal. I had asked for any spirits in the building to make a noticeable sound or activate an array. We had no success with communication during the session. After almost an hour, we concluded the session and moved all the equipment back into the room.

Ashley was lying on the bed and I was standing next to her, talking about the rest of the night's events. She was going through her camera bag.

"We won't be able to get any more pictures once the battery to the camera's gone, since I forgot the charger at home," she said.

"That's okay. We can get more pictures when we return."

We conversed for about another fifteen minutes, and my eyes started to wonder around the bed. There something lying next to Ashley.

"What's that?" I asked.

"The battery charger! It wasn't there before—I took everything out of the bag, and it wasn't in there," she explained. I can't say for sure where it came from, but I do know it appeared out of nowhere.

We then proceeded with another interactive session in our room. I placed the arrays around the room and put the Trifield meter in the center of the room. The lights were extinguished and the session began. We tried to contact Cornelia

Gayle, the young daughter of Clark Woodruff who is said to have died from the poison in the birthday cake made by Chloe. I called to her several times and received no response. I then asked if any other children were present and if they could try to communicate with us. Again, we documented no response. We continued for an hour and then closed the investigation for the evening, going to sleep shortly thereafter.

The next day we ended up meeting Glen, the general manager of the Myrtles Plantation, who invited us to lunch. We introduced ourselves and had a friendly discussion over lunch about the Myrtles in general as well as the ghostly reports and legends of the plantation. He explained to us about the occurrences that take place from time to time and how he would often find a set of keys lying in front of the door to the gift shop and an empty house in the morning. Apparently, the guests get frightened during the night and leave without staying to check out. I had heard a similar story about a couple who was staying at the Myrtles when they were frightened by something in the house and made their way to their car. When they discovered they left their car keys in the room, they decided to sleep outside in the pouring rain. I don't know if this is a true story or not, but it was one I came across while researching the plantation.

Glen continued to talk about the house, and we continued eating the delicious lunch. We thanked him for his time and the meal and then went on our way to another city for some sightseeing. We made a trip to Baton Rouge, grabbed dinner, and then returned to the Myrtles for the evening events. We booked two spots on the ghost tour of the house, which recounted the history of the Myrtles as well as the ghostly encounters that were reported. The tour took us through the entire house, which we did not have access to prior. We spoke briefly with the tour guide and made our way out of the main house and back into our new bedroom, the Fannie Williams Room. I was interested to see what type of activity we could encounter here.

This room was also located on the second floor. There was a queen bed and several dolls placed throughout the room. We had heard on the tour that the dolls in the room were of interest. Apparently, they would move by themselves and relocate at will. We placed arrays near the dolls as well as an audio recorder in the room in the hopes of capturing EVP. It was more difficult to do this with guests in the other rooms: there would be outside noise contamination from guests in adjacent rooms (yes, you can hear your neighbor).

I began asking questions to any spirits that may be in the room or in the area and invited them into our room. "Due to the noisiness of the floor, could you please move something or activate an array once you are in the room so we'll know you're here?" We did not get a response. I took it a step further and asked, "Will you move one of the dolls or throw one across the room?" Again, no response. We went through the normal proceedings for communication with no success.

Final Thoughts on the Myrtles Plantation

In conclusion, I would have to say that it is possible the Myrtles could be haunted, but we didn't experience anything while we were there. I went through the audio and did not find any evidence of EVP. We didn't receive any EMF spikes or changes. We could have been at the right place at the wrong time.

I was told by the general manager that the house is more active during thunderstorms, and a woman at the local McDonald's said when it rained, you could see little girls dancing outside in the yard of the plantation about six inches above the ground. This would also concur with the story of the couple that slept outside during the rainstorm.

Perhaps the Myrtles Plantation is some sort of an atmospheric haunting that has some connection with the energy in the area on certain days. I didn't pay to close attention to the moon phase or solar rays on that particular evening, but I don't feel they had any relevance to the haunting.

I would like to go back to the Myrtles one day to explore its history and to try again to capture paranormal activity. It was a very friendly environment. I would suggest anyone try the Myrtles at least once. You might end up encountering something strange that you just can't explain.

Chapter 5

THE CRESCENT HOTEL

Eureka Springs, Arkansas

Built in 1886 by Powell Clayton, the luxurious Crescent Hotel cost $294,000 to construct and has served guests for over a hundred years. However, before the massive building was a hotel, it was Crescent College and Conservatory for Young Women as well as Norman Baker's Cancer Curing Hospital.

From 1937 to 1939, the Crescent Hotel was host to dark and vile experiences that could account for all the paranormal activity that resides there today. A man named Norman Baker purchased the hotel in 1937 for the purpose of scamming money from people with cancer by claiming he had the cure. Though Baker had no formal education or licensure in medicine, he posed as a doctor, offering his services to cure people of the deadly disease. Many people fell victim to Baker's scheme and during his reign at the hospital, it is approximated that he made over four million dollars from his unsuspecting patients.

Eventually, his crimes caught up with him, and in 1940 he was convicted of mail fraud. The notorious Baker was sentenced to prison for four years and was fined four thousand dollars. He died in Florida in 1958 of liver cancer.

Today, the Crescent Hotel is a hot spot for tourists and paranormal investigators hoping to capture a glimpse of the afterlife. Many stories and rumors surround the hotel and its resident ghosts. One of the most popular ghosts in the hotel is the ghost of an Irish stonemason who fell to his death and landed in room 218. This room is said to be the most haunted room in the entire hotel. Some of the stories surrounding the haunting include apparitions of a man seen in the room as well as strange noises and the feeling of being watched. People refer to this spirit as "Michael." Michael likes to pull several tricks on the unsuspecting guests who stay in the room. Turning the lights on and off, banging on the walls, and turning the television on and off are a few of the phenomena that have been reported by eyewitnesses who have stayed overnight in room 218.

Another famously haunted room is 419. A woman named Theodora is said to move things around the room when guests are disruptive and very angry, particularly when it comes to people who drink a lot of alcohol. This room is said to be another hot spot for EVP as well. Other spirits that have been seen and heard include a man in the downstairs women's bathroom, a small female child, and Dr. Ellis. Some people have also claimed the spirit of Norman Baker himself is in the Crescent Hotel basement.

First Investigation: The Basement Comes Alive

I have visited the Crescent Hotel on several occasions and conducted paranormal investigations, getting what I felt to be confirmation that the spirits of the building were still there. In fact, I have frequented the Crescent Hotel more than any other out-of-state location. On my first investigation of the building, I went up to the hotel around Labor Day 2005. I was still the director of my first paranormal team, and Phillip, a long-time friend and researcher, accompanied me for the duration of my stay. As we drove up to the Crescent from St. Louis, I told him the stories about the Crescent's restless ghosts that haunt the hotel.

When we arrived in Eureka Springs, it took us a while to locate the road going up to the Crescent Hotel. In fact, it took several stops at gas stations and restaurants before we got a map of the town and accurate directions. Once we had arrived at the hotel, we checked in and took all our equipment up to room 218, where we would be staying the two nights we were there. The room was fairly standard to that of any other rooms in the hotel. It was smaller in the fact that there was one bed and window. Once the unpacking was completed and our equipment was set up, I had told Phillip, who was in the bathroom at the time, that I was going outside to get something out of the car and I would be right back. He said he was going to take a shower and clean up for the investigation. I went down to the car to retrieve the piece of equipment I forgot and brought it up to the room. By this point, Phillip was out of the bathroom and standing next to the bed.

"Did you come back in at any time after you left? I thought you might have forgotten your keys or something," he said.

"No, I didn't reenter the room until I had the equipment," I told him.

"About sixty seconds after I heard you leave the room and the door close, I heard footsteps walking around the room." He had called out to me had gotten no response. When he walked out of the bathroom, he had expected to see me in the room, only I was still downstairs.

Seeing that it was a few hours before the start of the ghost tour and we hadn't eaten in hours, we headed into town to find someplace to eat and came back to the hotel for the daily ghost tour.

If we were going to investigate, we wanted to have as much knowledge about the activity as possible, and I was told by the guests and staff that the tour was very informative about the history of the Crescent as well as the ghosts. Before the tour started, we met a newlywed couple that was on their honeymoon at the Crescent (which is notorious for weddings and receptions as well). They had asked if we could take them along on our investigation at some point, and we agreed to meet up after the tour.

One of the last places we were taken on the tour was the Crescent basement. This would be a great place to start, given all the sightings and experiences down there. Also, the basement was once used as a morgue when the building was a hospital. We asked an employee if we could gain access for an hour or so to investigate. He agreed to give us some time in the basement, and we felt this would be a great experience for our newlywed friends as well.

Phillip and I met up with the couple and escorted them to the basement of the building. The basement was fairly large. There were two rooms connected to each other with a third (storage) room off to the side. The first (main) room of the basement had a large storage freezer compartment with what appeared to be a morgue table next to it. We set up the camcorder, extinguished all the lights, and sat down. I decided to go into a separate room to see if I could cause a response. Down the hall at the other end of the basement, there was a room that looked like it was used for woodwork and such. It also had a door leading to the outside of the building. As I stood in the center of the dark and cold room, I sensed a presence to my left.

I asked out loud, "If there is anyone in this room, will you please make a noise so I can know where you are?" About two seconds later, I heard a distinct, loud bang on what I thought to be a pipe: it was metal to metal contact, like a wrench hitting a pipe. I thanked whoever made the noise and kept asking for responses. Moments passed without noise, so I headed over to the side basement room, where Baker had kept body organs in glass jars. The area was now used for storage, holding bolts, screws, and so on. I stayed in the room for about ten minutes with nothing to report and then decided to rejoin the rest of the group.

As I made my way through the doorway, I looked to my right and noticed that all three of the other group members were looking upward at something. They had very confused looks on their faces.

I walked over to Phillip and asked, "What's going on?" Before he could answer, I looked up saw several long wooden boards set above the hallway. The boards were moving up and down as if someone were shaking them.

Phillip asked, "Logan, can you give me a rational explanation for why those boards are moving?"

I could not answer him. I grabbed a chair, and Phillip got up to check for a rodent or some air current, finding neither. There was no vibration coming from the area the boards were lying on. We had absolutely no evidence to support a rational cause of the movement of the boards. We decided to do a sit-down session in the main basement area. We did not hear any responses or noises to validate that someone was there or willing to communicate.

As we were about to leave, one of the newlyweds jumped forward about six feet. Curious, I asked why he made such a sudden movement, and I could see that he was visually shaken. He kept holding his right arm.

"Someone or something grabbed the side of my arm as I was getting up," he explained. I grabbed the infrared (IR) thermometer and started taking readings on his arm. In a small area on his arm, where he claimed he was grabbed, I measured a ten-degree difference from the rest of his arm. I waited a few minutes to see if whoever grabbed him would give us a confirmation by making a noise, but we heard nothing. We quickly exited the basement area and proceeded back to the main building and to our rooms. Our guests turned in for the night, and Phillip and I explored the outside of the building.

It was a very beautiful building in daylight and even more beautiful in darkness. The gardens of the hotel were attractive. The long walking trail, surrounded by numerous flowers and trees, led down to the main street. Phillip and I started walking through the gardens of the Crescent when I noticed a woman in a white gown dart off to the left at the steps at the end of the trail we were walking on. I started walking fast to see if I could catch her and told myself that I didn't just see a ghost. It wouldn't be the first time I had seen an apparition, but I wanted an explanation. When I approached the end of the trail, I looked around but found no one. It was dead silent. Puzzled, I tried to figure out what could have just happened.

I later found out about a woman who had been seen peeking through the windows at people and was also spotted in the gardens. Supposedly, the woman fell from the roof of the building. No one really knows if she was pushed or if it was a suicide. Either way, she is one of the resident ghosts of the Crescent

Hotel. There were some instances when people called the police to say they saw a woman fall from the top of the Crescent Hotel.

Exhausted from the trip over and the investigation, we decided to call it a night and retire to our room. The next day we got up fairly early and explored downtown Eureka Springs. This is one of the highlights of investigating here because of all the unique shops and restaurants. We had lunch and took a quick tour of the Basin Park Hotel, which is the sister property of the Crescent Hotel and is rumored to be haunted as well. After lunch, we met two young women who were visiting the hotel from a different city in Arkansas. We spoke briefly with them and promised to take them around later that evening for a tour of the various haunted locations.

When the time came to start the tour and investigation, Phillip and one of the women were missing. The other woman and I waited about ten minutes and decided to start without them. We made our first stop in the basement, waiting a few minutes to hear or see anything. We heard several unexplained noises and knocks but had to move to a different location due to our missing people and our schedule. I took my guest through the garden to see if we could experience anything like Phillip and I had the night before.

As we approached the trail, I could see a series of lights flashing up ahead. I first thought it was people with flashlights looking for ghosts.

"I guess we are not the only ones looking for ghosts tonight," I said. We made our way farther down the trail, and I saw that no one was there. No car drove off, and there was no one in sight.

We eventually met up with Phillip and the other woman, and all four of us went up to the North Penthouse Suite, which was Norman Baker's apartment. During our stay, we heard several knocks and noises coming from inside the room. These noises appeared to be random and not direct communication.

When the girls decided to retire, Phillip and I sat in the main living area and chatted for a bit with the video camera running. The room was large with several chairs and a sink area across the room. We started hearing the same noises we had heard earlier with the guests. Phillip was skeptical about the noises, passing them off as wind or the hotel settling. As he spoke, the noises got louder and more frequent. Then, after about five minutes of silence, there was a huge crash. There was so much force that it sounded like someone had knocked over a refrigerator.

I jumped in my chair and exclaimed, "What the hell was that?!"

"The wind?" Phillip said.

A bit later we were still seated in the living area. There was a sink in the area right in front of us. On the sink was a squeezable glow-in-the-dark ghost that the Crescent would give you if you stayed the night. Well, due to the light being on earlier, the ghost was glowing, and I could see the reflection of the ghost in the mirror by the sink. The ghost, very slowly, started sliding on the countertop it was on. I confirmed the movement with the reflection in the mirror as well. When the ghost reached near the end of the counter, it jumped off—it wasn't thrown off, nor did it fall. It made a small jump off the counter and onto the floor. I asked Phillip if he saw it, and he confirmed.

We also investigated inside the crystal dining room. Phillip and I heard what sounded like plates hitting the table and silverware bouncing off the floor. I was so convinced that someone was messing around back there that I told the man stationed at the front desk that he should go back there and see if someone had slipped back there to do something. The front desk clerk made his way through the kitchen and came back with a sandwich.

"What the hell?" I asked.

"There was no one back there and nothing seemed disturbed," the clerk said. After a short while, we returned to our room and we went to sleep.

The next day we got up and started packing for the ride home. We made one last tour of the hotel and talked to a few employees about the experiences. Overall, I was very pleased with our results from on the first trip. We walked away with a few EVP as well as all the personal experiences.

The second-floor hallway of the Crescent Hotel.

Second Investigation:
The Man at the Dining Room Table

I knew the first chance I got I would be returning to the hotel for more investigating, and less than a year later, I came back. My second trip was less eventful but still interesting. I planned a trip to the hotel with several other investigators because they had never been there before. Brandon and I, along with Albert and Penny from the St. James investigation, made the drive to see what we could document in the haunted hotel.

One of the unique things about this trip was the opportunity to produce the first webcam show of the Crescent Hotel. We took our website viewers on a live tour of the hotel, and they got to investigate with us. The tour went extremely well, and the most exciting part of the investigation was when we conducted a sweep of the crystal dining room. This is a very large ballroom-sized restaurant with multiple tables and chairs throughout. The large windows provide plenty of light throughout the day. A bar area and piano also accompany the room. Albert got a considerable temperature reading in one of the chairs at a table. The infrared thermometer registered a reading of 57 degrees, while the rest of the chairs were 67 to 68 degrees. He checked the temperature of the chair a second time and it went back up to 68 degrees.

Shortly after that, I was documenting things in my notebook and looked up to see a figure go through what I thought to be one of the doorways and disappear. When I went over to examine the doorway, I saw that it wasn't a doorway the figure went into—it was a window.

A man is said to haunt the crystal dining room. There are eyewitness accounts of a man sitting at the table, waiting for a woman that he had met at a dance or party. The man didn't have the courage to ask the woman to dance and was waiting for her to return to do so. She apparently died in a car accident before she came back, and the man forever haunts the dining room, waiting for her.

All these experiences are very similar to ones many guests over the years have witnessed. *Why are they happening, and how do we validate that they are something spiritual?* I thought. It was clear to me that there was historical evidence to support some of the hauntings, though I was not yet aware what could be triggering these events. Were some of them residual hauntings that took place at a certain time or location? Were there specific intelligent spirits that were causing multiple events? These were the questions I was seeking answers to, and with that, I planned another trip to the hotel.

Third Investigation:
The Spirit of Joe and Voices Beckoning

On January 26, 2007, I took yet another trip to the Crescent Hotel to document any and all occurrences that appeared to be paranormal or unexplained. I called ahead and made reservations for Ashley and me for rooms 419 and 502. These were the only two rooms in the hotel reported to have activity that I had not yet stayed in.

Ashley and I arrived in Eureka Springs around five thirty in the evening, and the bell captain took our equipment and luggage up to room 419. We decided to head to town to get some dinner and come back. Upon our return around seven thirty, I stopped by the ghost tour office to see if Carroll was there so I could speak with him. He was not at the hotel during my previous trip, and I wanted to ask him a few questions about the ghostly history of the hotel. I met Carroll back in September 2005 when I made my very first trip to the Crescent with Phillip. I spoke briefly with Carroll, who was leaving before the ghost tour for that evening began, and told him that I would be in contact with him via email.

We decided to take the ghost tour that night since this was Ashley's first time at the Crescent and I needed a refresher on the spirits of the building. Brian was our tour guide for the evening. We made our rounds throughout the building, and Brian recounted the experiences that the guests have had over the years. I was familiar with the history of most of the rooms from my past visits (218 on the first trip and 313 on the second). There were, however, some things that I was shocked to learn, and the stories had some relation to the evidence that we had collected on a previous trip. Brian explained about Joe, a friend of his who had worked in the kitchen area. Joe witnessed a glass hover over the sink and then fall into the sink and break.

After the ghost tour, we headed down to the basement of the Crescent, which was once the morgue area. The tour guide had mentioned Raymond, a spirit who would pull on the jewelry of the female guests who came down to the basement. After exploring a bit, we headed back up to the room to get the equipment for the first investigation of the basement. A staff member named Boyd escorted us to the basement and locked the door to make sure that no one else could get in. We set up our stationary arrays throughout the main room with the freezer (in which Baker kept bodies) and the morgue table. We placed another array in the doorway to the parts room, one in the doorway to the back room, and one on the chair by the desk in the office area of the basement. We turned off all the lights and sat in chairs next to each other in front of the freezer door. I started the audio recorder to run EVP and had my digital camera ready to capture a picture or two.

I started off asking the spirits to let us know if they were in the room or the nearby area by making a noise or setting off an array. There was no response.

"Is the spirit known as Raymond present?" Ashley asked. "He is welcome to pull on my necklace or earrings if he wishes." Still there was no response.

I went next. "Is the spirit Joe?"

Right after I spoke those words, the array sitting on the morgue table started flashing at one milligauss, a significantly low reading but strong enough to indicate a disruption in the field.

"Is Joe the one doing that?" The array became activated at a solid one.

"Can Joe make the array spike higher than a one?" Nothing happened. "Brian was down in the basement earlier and had mentioned Joe on the ghost tour." Still the array was at a solid one.

After about five or ten minutes of trying to get the array to go higher, I asked if the spirit could please step away from the meter and make it go back down to zero. No response.

After another five to ten minutes, Ashley turned the meter off and back on. If there was an issue with the battery or with the meter itself, it should not come back on as a solid one. She power cycled the meter, and it was still at a solid one. I asked her to pick the meter up, and she picked it up and moved it around the table. It was still lighting up, so it was apparent that the table itself was charged somehow. I asked her to place the meter on the floor in front of the table, and it did not activate on the floor.

We continued with our investigation of the basement, running audio for EVP and asking questions to get a meter activation. Around eleven thirty the bell captain came down and told us that we had to wrap up for the evening.

We packed our gear up and made our way back to room 419. This is a very open room, almost two rooms in one. There is a sitting area as you first walk in with a couch and chair. The second area has a large bed and bathroom. These areas are divided by a large opening. Once we entered the room, we sat our equipment down and got into bed. A spirit called Theodora has been seen around the room, and some guests had even reported hearing her voice from within the room. I set up arrays throughout the room including the living room area. With all lights extinguished, I could easily see the array pilot lights illuminating both rooms. I continued asking questions to solicit a response, some of which were directed at Theodora. We had heard that she did not like yelling and fighting amongst couples, so Ashley and I thought about possibly creating a fake negative interaction as research to see if that would make something happen but then decided against it. We finally became tired, turned off the Trifield meter and the arrays, and went to bed for the evening.

I remember lying there before I fell asleep, thinking, *What is it about this room that makes it so haunted?* I had not heard one single strange noise or had anything bizarre happen. I wondered if it was just one of those nights that no matter where you go, you just don't get anything to happen.

I fell asleep not too long after, only to wake several hours later from a startling nightmare. I found myself in the pitch dark living room area, standing in the center of the room. *How the hell did I wind up in here?* I felt my way through the dark room and into the bathroom to get a drink of water from the sink. I didn't move right away; I just stared into the mirror trying to figure out what had happened. This wasn't the first time that I had a bad experience with a haunted room while I was asleep. After about five minutes in the bathroom, I made my way back to Ashley and the bed and went back to sleep.

I woke up the next morning and got things packed for the move to room 502, which is now the North Penthouse Suite. This same room was once Norman Baker's apartment. I reserved the room after having the experience with Phillip on my first visit to the Crescent, and I thought Ashley would appreciate the view and the roominess of the suite. Once we walked in the door, we went up the stairs to the room, which was very large and open. The windows, once open, created a large panoramic view of the Ozark Mountains. This was in fact the highest elevated spot in the city.

As we were moving in our luggage and unpacking, I was in the living area of the room. I heard a voice but couldn't distinguish what it said. It came from up the stairs.

"Did you say something?" I asked. She said no, and that was that. I was puzzled and told her I thought she was upstairs asking me something.

After the move, we went to town to eat and came back for our afternoon spa appointment. The rest of the day was spent in Eureka Springs searching through the downtown shops for souvenirs. We returned to the hotel shortly after dinner and prepared to return to the basement.

For this trip we met Tony and Deanna at the hotel. We invited them to the basement for a lesson on how we conduct investigations. Ashley and I went back down alone at first. Boyd let us in and made sure we were okay. We began the setup and placed the EMF arrays around the main room. We started asking questions and but heard no response.

A short time later, Tony and Deanna came down, escorted by Boyd, and we moved into the back room. With arrays in place, we sat down and started collecting data. We had audio recorders going and took photographs and temperature readings as well.

"If any spirits are present, could you please make yourselves known by making a noise, moving something, or activating an array?" I asked. Gathering no positive results, we finished up and returned to our rooms.

Naturally, I was eager to make my way to bed upstairs. We retired for the evening, and I made my way to the bathroom for about two minutes and then started on my way up the staircase.

About halfway up, Ashley asked, "What did you say?"

"I didn't say anything."

She claimed as I made my way up the stairs there was a voice that mumbled something on the staircase, and she thought it was me. I again assured her that I didn't say anything, but I remembered hearing a voice on the stairs earlier in the day as well. We headed to bed and then checked out the next day.

Fourth Investigation: The Eye under the Bed

My most recent stay in the Crescent Hotel took place in December 2009. There were four investigators going, including me and Cathy. We arrived at the hotel in hopes of getting room 218, only to find out it was booked. We ended up getting room 426 instead, which was good because I had not been in the room, and it would be a new experience to me.

In the room, we set up a camera that would be recording around the clock. Everyone went on the ghost tour, and at the conclusion we ended up in the room trying to interact with anyone that could be in there. We continued investigating, and Cathy began taking photographs around the room at about two in the morning. We had various EMF arrays and detectors placed throughout the room. As we asked for any spirits or entities to reveal themselves, no one came forward, and we continued waiting throughout the night. It was well after three in the morning when we finally went to sleep.

We woke up a few hours later and started back for Oklahoma. Upon evidence review, we did identify an anomaly in one of the photographs Cathy captured with her phone. You can easily see something manifested at the foot of the bed. When we further analyzed the photo, I realized that it was a human eye looking out of the bed. I couldn't tell if it was something appearing or going away, but it was an interesting photo to say the least.

Final Thoughts on the Crescent Hotel

I have had many unique experiences in the Crescent Hotel and plan to have many more. It is one of the more intriguing and affordable places to visit. I try to take one to two trips a year there to visit the town and the hotel. It is, however, one of the more difficult places to investigate due to the constant noise from people going up and down the halls as well as the weddings and receptions that are a frequent occurrence.

The one thing I could suggest is to book a haunted room and spend some time in it after hours when everyone else has gone to bed. If you can, also spend some time in the basement alone, as I feel this is one of the focal points of the activity.

Bring a good amount of equipment to try to document activity. If you are willing to spend the time and money, you just might find that there are paranormal encounters waiting around every corner.

Chapter 6

ƒEFFERSON, TEXAS

There is a town just fifteen miles north of Marshall, Texas, that is rumored to be the most haunted town in Texas. Jefferson, Texas, is very historic and small, but there is a number of haunted locations within it. So many, in fact, that the city has a public ghost tour to most of the haunted locations on a weekly basis and a semiannual paranormal conference (usually held in April and November) that brings ghost hunters from around the area together to share in the events. I first ended up there wanting to know more about the town and its paranormal past. There are two key places within the town that I have investigated for paranormal activity. The first one on the list is probably the most famous: the Jefferson Hotel.

The Jefferson Hotel

By the look of it, you wouldn't guess this building is one of the most haunted places in the United States. The hotel does not have a violent past or any other obvious reason for why it would be so haunted to this day. The building was constructed in 1851 and used as a cotton gin. After the gin shut down, it became the Crystal Ballroom, and later it was converted into the Jefferson Hotel. Over the years the hotel has been in business, many guests have reported many different types of paranormal phenomena in several different rooms of the hotel. I had the pleasure of sleeping in several of them.

The Jefferson Hotel.

First Investigation: The Awakening

My first visit to the hotel was January 1, 2006. I had reservations to stay for two nights in room 19, which was the most active room according to the hotel guests and staff. I would not be alone on this trip, for Brandon decided to accompany me to the hotel.

After the long drive to Jefferson, we unpacked and talked to a few members of the cleaning staff. Then we swept the hotel for EMF and temperature anomalies. In room 4, I asked our cleaning-crew friend who went with us if there were any stories about children in this room, and she told me a story about children's handprints on the window. I went into the bathroom and got several high EMF readings in the center of the room. I didn't move, yet the readings would go from low to high in almost a pulsating motion. We left the room and proceeded to the next room. In room 5, I got an EMF spike next to the first bed that lasted about two to three minutes.

Room 18 at the Jefferson Hotel.

We made our way back to room 19, and I napped for a bit before we started the investigation. I awoke to Brandon sitting in the chair of our room.

"What did I miss?" I asked.

"When you went to bed, I decided to take a bath," he explained. "While I was in the tub, I could hear a conversation going on in the room next to us. After the bath, I headed out to get some footage for the video we were making." He made a stop by the front desk and found out that the room next to us, room 18, was unoccupied and no one was in there. So, the voice he was hearing in the tub was coming from an empty room.

Even stranger was when he returned: "As I opened the door and started to make my way in, you sat up in bed and reached out to me, saying things I couldn't understand. After about eight seconds, you lay back down and were immediately asleep." Now, some people would think that I was just actively dreaming, and it was some part of my unconscious coming out to say hello. Another theory is that it was a form of xenoglossy. Xenoglossy is the ability to speak or write in other languages that have not been learned by the speaker. This can be associated with a trance state. And then, of course, there is also the theory of possession. Whatever the phenomenon was, I think Brandon was a little bothered by it.

Later that night, we felt it would be best to contain our activity to our room and not travel the hotel floor. The room was small with one full-size bed. There was a lamp next to the bed and chandelier light above it. The bathroom was standard with a mirror that was supposed to exhibit paranormal activity. To conduct our research, we sat in the dark with the camera running and monitored activity. Suddenly, we heard a clicking sound. We didn't know what it was at first until we examined the camera. Something or someone unseen by us turned the camera completely off. I turned the camera back on and verified that it was working properly (strong battery, new tape). We documented the event and didn't get much communication other than some unexplained noises, so we decided to go to bed for the night.

The next day we got up and headed to my hometown of Shreveport to get something to eat and entertain ourselves until nightfall. We took Jefferson's local ghost tour after dinner, which led us around the town to a few of the places that were haunted. At the conclusion, we reentered the hotel and decided to sweep the entire building. Before we left our room, we shut and locked the door to make sure our things would be safe inside. I verified this by checking the knob to see if it was locked.

We started the sweep on the bottom floor and went throughout the hallways. We did not have access to any of the other guest rooms, so we only investigated the lobby, stairs, and hallways. We used a Cell Sensor EMF, EVP audio recorders, and IR thermometers. No paranormal readings or occurrences were documented.

When we returned to the room, the door was wide open. I walked up and checked the knob, and it was still locked. At first I thought I maybe didn't shut it all the way, but it would have swung open earlier if that were the case. Then I checked the locking mechanism to see if there was a defect that might release the latch and allow the door to open even though it was still technically locked. I couldn't find that either. We made a check of our equipment and personal belongings just to make sure nothing was missing. Everything in the room was untouched. We decided to start another sit-down session in the room.

During the second night's investigation, I sensed something negative in our room. It came over me very suddenly and was very obvious. Brandon saw the room get darker all of a sudden, but it didn't last long. We heard no responses to our questions nor did any equipment activate. We ended up going to bed shortly after.

The next morning, we got up and packed the car. I spoke with one of the managers of the hotel. We briefly spoke of the events that took place, and I told her I would be coming back soon and with more people. One month later, I did just that.

Second Investigation: Who Was in Room 1?

In February 2006, I returned to the Jefferson Hotel. This time I had Albert and Penny with me as well as Brandon. We unpacked the car and set the equipment up in the room. We stayed in room 5 on this trip, which had two queen beds and a lamp. As we were roaming the hotel, we were fortunate enough this time to meet some other guests who were more than willing for us to come into their room and investigate. One of those rooms was room 1.

Room 1 was very similar to room 5 with two queen beds. We entered the room and placed EMF arrays throughout. There were two people sitting on one bed and Albert and Penny sitting on another. We placed one array on the nightstand next to the bed. On numerous occasions, this array would go off in response to questions.

"Are there any spirits present?" I asked, and the array would go off.

"Is there was some way we could help you?" Again, the array activated. We also captured this on film. At several points, we heard knocking-sound responses to questions, and some of the guests felt strange or uncomfortable in the room. When we asked aloud if the spirits were going to stay in the room tonight and interact with the guests, there was a large bang in the corner of the room. One of the guests staying in the room that night got up and left the room. I'm not sure if they came back to stay in the room that night or not, but I know I did not see them the rest of the trip. We concluded investigating in room 1 and made our way back to our own room.

It wasn't long before there was a knock on the door. There stood a young woman whom I had talked to earlier and who was staying in room 19, which I stayed in with Brandon last month. She asked if I had time to come back to her room and talk to her for a while about the activity. She also wanted my expert opinion on some things that she had experienced in the past. I followed her back to room 19, and she told me stories about growing up and about some of the things that interested her about the paranormal, thus bringing her to the hotel. I told her about my prior experiences in room 19 and how some things are reoccurring and some are sporadic in nature.

The hallway on the second floor of the Jefferson Hotel.

As we talked, we started hearing some sounds on the wall by the window. Not long after, we began hearing noises that sounded as if someone were walking on the floor. I even put my ear to the ground and verified I was hearing the noises. At one point, I could even feel floor movement, but nothing was there. I continued talking with the girl for a few more hours and then walked back to the room and went to bed.

We got up early the next morning and then headed home that day.

Third Investigation: Third Time Is Not a Charm

In January 2007, I returned to Jefferson with Ashley and investigated the hotel once more. We arrived on January 13 and checked into room 19 once again. Ashley had never been to the hotel, and I thought it would be a good time to give her a lesson on the hotel's haunted history.

Before we could even get settled, things started to happen. I went into the bathroom of the room for a short minute. When I exited, Ashley pointed out the chandelier in the room was moving. There was no air current in the room and no vibrations to indicate it should have been swinging like it was. Shortly after, we both heard voices whispering in the room.

Later that night, we both were inside the room doing interactive sessions. We decided to take a break, and I walked downstairs to grab a soda from the vending machine on the first floor. The arrays were still in place and turned on. When I returned to the room, she told me that while I was gone, the array that was on the floor of the room had activated several times.

I was convinced I could get some good EVP or photographic evidence in the room but didn't. I tried asking if the spirits would manifest themselves in the room. I started surveying the room for shadows and would occasionally take pictures to see if I could capture evidence of a manifestation. I did not capture any. I tried doing knock tests and asking if the spirits could move a door or perhaps furniture. Nothing responded and nothing was moved. It wasn't long before we concluded the investigation and went to sleep.

We checked out the next day, but I was not disappointed that I didn't get much activity because I knew I would be coming back in the following month. On the way out, I verified my reservation and drove back to Oklahoma.

Fourth Investigation: The Jacuzzi Room

The fourth time I took the opportunity to visit the Jefferson Hotel was on February 7, one day before my twenty-eighth birthday. Ashley and I stopped in Jefferson on the way to the Myrtles Plantation. I wanted to stay in room 25 since I hadn't stayed in the room yet and thought this would be a good opportunity to have new experiences. The room had one large king bed and a small sitting area. The room also had a Jacuzzi tub, and I wanted to make the most of the night.

We did a small investigation that night in which the EMF meter went off as I was approaching the living area from the bed. It was almost like someone was backing up as I was walking toward them.

In the bathroom, I had a strange incident with a bath towel that kept ending up on the floor. At first I thought it was multiple towels, but I ended up marking one with water and verifying it was the same towel that was getting misplaced. We ended up going to sleep shortly thereafter, and the next day we packed up and headed to the Myrtles.

Final Thoughts on the Jefferson Hotel

The Jefferson Hotel is one of the most comfortable and relaxing haunted locations I have ever visited. It's almost like small-town life, without the chaos of big-city living. Everyone there is very hospitable. All the other guests we have come across have been very willing to learn and friendly.

Another great thing about the hotel is the affordability of the rooms. They run specials through the week if you wish to stay more than one night. I'm not saying it's the most haunted place I have been, but I have never had a problem there with the staff or doing investigations. Of the town's paranormal offerings, it is definitely one not to be missed.

The Excelsior House

The Excelsior House is an old historic hotel much like the Jefferson Hotel but not as eager to discuss its haunted reputation. I first learned about the Excelsior House during the public ghost tour. The tour guide stopped us outside the hotel and told us about the "famous" Steven Spielberg event that happened sometime in the eighties.

According to the legend, Spielberg stayed at the hotel many years ago in the room that is now known as the Jay Gould Room. He arrived in the room and threw his briefcase in the small rocking chair that is still in the room to this day. The chair apparently threw the briefcase back at him. During the night, he was awakened by a small boy at the foot of his bed who promptly asked him if he wanted some breakfast. Spielberg apparently checked out of the hotel and has not returned.

I heard other stories about paranormal activity in other rooms at the hotel. Some of these stories were about people getting locked into rooms and people being chased out of the hotel by an unseen force. One in particular came from a former employee who said that one night she was making her rounds in the building to close up and came in contact with an entity that was making it difficult to open one of the doors. She said the doorknob would turn and move but when she tried to open it, someone on the other side of the door was preventing it from opening. After she struggled with the opposing force for a few minutes, the door finally opened. There was no one in the room, and it was dark.

Investigating the Excelsior House: Get Out of My Chair!

Ashley and I traveled to Jefferson, Texas, on February 10, 2007, on our way back from the Myrtles Plantation. I decided to book a historic room at the Excelsior House since I had not stayed there before, and I felt Ashley would be intrigued by the history of the hotel—not to mention it's supposed to be really haunted. I booked the Jay Gould room for one night, and once we arrived, we promptly took our bags up to the room. Although I wasn't sure if I could believe the Spielberg story, I thought it would be interesting to take the opportunity to check the hotel out for myself. It wasn't long before things started happening.

I went outside to get some things out of the trunk of the car, and Ashley opted to stay in the room. She had stepped outside to talk briefly with another guest who was staying in a different room. When she returned inside the room, her camera was on one side of the bed and the lens cap was on the other. While she thought it was strange, she placed the cap back on the camera and the camera back into the bag. I returned to the room with the remainder of the luggage, and she told me about the events that had taken place. I didn't think too much about it at the time and started getting things out of our bags.

The room has a very authentic feel to it. Large drapes, a chandelier, antique looking lamps, rugs, and a single rocking chair adorned this room. There were two beds, both the same size. As I was on one of them, I took a quick glance across the room and noticed one of the windows had the shade up. I looked outside and could clearly see the street corner and people near it. I thought to myself, *Wow, someone could be standing there watching us right now. I guess I should have pulled the shade down when I entered the room.* I sat up in bed and took another look around the room.

I was a little disoriented at first, but I soon realized that the shade had been pulled down to the bottom of the window. Furthermore, neither of us heard anything moving inside the room prior to this happening. I went to examine the shade at the window. The shade was very old, and the roller at the top of the window would squeak anytime the shade was pulled up or down. I tried several different times, both slow and fast, but still heard the squeaking noise. I decided just for safety's sake to check the door. The door was still securely locked, and nothing else was moved.

Ashley and I jumped in the shower real fast before continuing with the day. We heard a small noise or two from inside the room when we were showering but nothing significant. When we got out, Ashley decided she was going to blow dry her hair. I got dressed and told her I was heading down to the coffee shop with my laptop to access the internet and check email. I walked out the door and made sure it was locked. I made my way next door to the coffee shop and hopped on the internet for about ten minutes before deciding to head back to the hotel.

I opened the room and walked back in. Ashley was still in the bathroom using the blow dryer. I set my laptop down on the floor by the bed and sat down. We engaged in some short conversation, and I once again started looking around the room. In the corner by the window, I noticed a strange difference. The rocking chair—yes, the same one referenced in the Spielberg story—had moved. Once facing inside the room, it now faced out toward the window, as if someone moved it to look outside.

"Ashley, did you move anything in the room?" I didn't tell her what I was referencing; I just asked if she moved anything.

"No. Since you left, I haven't left the bathroom," she replied. I took note of the events, and we continued on with the day.

We took the afternoon to visit neighboring Marshall for dinner with the stuttering waiter. We decided to head back to Jefferson and once again attend the ghost tour, a special experience in itself. We always enjoyed the tour and go every opportunity we have. After the tour, we decided to head back to the room and finish the night. Before we went to bed I set all the EMF arrays around the room with fresh batteries and the EMF meter on a dresser in front of us. All the meters were on and I had an audio recorder going as well. Ashley fell asleep, and I started asking questions to see if I could get a response. I was unsuccessful.

About thirty to forty-five minutes later I myself fell asleep. I woke up and looked around the room. I noticed that all the EMF arrays except one were dimly lit and almost completely depleted in battery. The one EMF array I placed on the rocking chair was going off. Something seemed to have caused it to activate at some time during the night. Whatever it was would have had to manifest at that particular location in order to cause only that meter to activate. If something would have moved to that location, it would have passed the other meters and caused them to also activate. The only thing I wish I had was a time stamp to indicate when the activation took place. Perhaps next time I will bring a device that logs time or has an audible alarm to register activations. Either way I felt it was an interesting occurrence. Nothing further was experienced on this trip. We got up the next morning and drove home.

Final Thoughts on the Excelsior House

I feel that there is definitely some type of paranormal activity at the Excelsior House. It is very rare to experience so many different types of things on your first time at a location. I can't help but wonder with the hotel being historic if some of the activity might be residual. It's obvious that there is an intelligent presence there, but I didn't spend enough time in enough places to make a more solid conclusion. When I return, I plan to access multiple rooms in the historic wing and compare the experiences to several others.

While the hotel management does not like paranormal investigations, I suggest that anyone stay a night or two at the Excelsior for a good chance of experiencing something unexplainable.

Final Thoughts on Jefferson, Texas

Overall, Jefferson is a very unique and quiet town with much to offer the paranormal community. There were several locations I did not get the privilege to investigate, including the Schluter home. If you find yourself in the area, take the time to visit this small town for the historic aspect if nothing else. The spirits of Jefferson seem to have a need to be known and recognized. It's almost like a hidden community within a community. It's a place where the spirits anticipate your arrival and eagerly await your return.

Chapter 7
GUTHRIE, OKLAHOMA

Just north of Oklahoma City lies the town of Guthrie. Much like Jefferson, Texas, Guthrie has had its fair share of reported ghosts and hauntings. Guthrie has a very long history, including being the former state capital of Oklahoma. While there are several places in Guthrie that are haunted, this chapter focuses on three key locations. I have had many personal experiences in these three places, and together these places make up the heart of this historic and haunted Oklahoma town.

The Stone Lion Inn

The Stone Lion Inn is probably the most well-known haunted bed-and-breakfast in the state of Oklahoma. The B and B is so well known in fact that it was first featured on national television in 2006. Its hauntings date back to early 1900s when a man named F. E. Houghton built the home for his family when they outgrew the home they currently lived in right next door. The Houghtons had many children, and one of them is thought to be the spirit living in the house today. It is rumored that when Augusta Houghton was eight years old, she passed away after being given the wrong medication for an illness. This was later disproven when the family history was researched and it was found that Augusta actually grew up and passed away in her later years in life. This did not change the general belief that there is a spirit of a child in the home, and to this day several things have been attributed to her presence.

The Stone Lion Inn.

In 1987 the home was purchased by its current owner, Becky Luker. She claims that during the time her family lived in the house, toys in the upstairs attic room would be constantly scattered about. Today the home is converted into a bed-and-breakfast, but that does not stop the ghostly spirits that reside within from interacting with the unfamiliar guests. Guests have reported to Luker that in one certain room late at night they feel like someone is patting their face with a small hand. Other accounts of reported activity include hearing children laughing, footsteps, and sightings of a male figure. I heard of the stories over the years and decided it was time to check out the house firsthand.

First Investigation: Video Recording Prohibited

In July of 2005, I first checked in to the Stone Lion as a guest. This trip, I was in the Lucille Mulhall Suite. I was given permission to conduct the investigation in the room if the other guests were not disturbed.

I met a young couple, Mike and Karen, who were staying in the hotel as well and were very interested in the paranormal. I spoke with them briefly about my past experiences and their interest in the paranormal. They agreed to let me in their room, the Cora Diehl Suite, to investigate. The room housed a full-size bed, and various articles of clothing were pinned and painted on the walls of the room. We sat around the bed asking questions to see if any spirits would respond. I placed several EMF meters around the room and waited in silence with the guests. After about forty-five minutes of no activity, we concluded the investigation of this room. After their room was complete, they followed me to the study and finally to my room.

When all was said and done, I thanked them for their assistance and said that I would be in touch with them. I entered the Lucille Mulhall Suite, which was a smaller room with a full-size bed and bathroom. I positioned my video camera to record toward the door to the room and climbed into bed. I lay there with my eyes closed for about two minutes until I heard a door open. I then felt a presence move closer to the bed, and a few seconds later the camera switched off all by itself. I opened my eyes halfway expecting to see someone standing by my bed near the camera. No one was there.

The Lucille Mulhall Suite in the Stone Lion Inn.

I didn't feel I had collected much evidence, so I was anxious to conduct a better investigation of the Stone Lion.

Second Investigation: The Ball and the Plate

In December of that year I set up another investigation with Penny, Albert, Jerico (a team member), and Brandon. Brandon and I decided to meet with Luker early in the day to get access to the inn for video shots. After meeting with Luker at her residence in Guthrie and obtaining the key, we then traveled to the house and started the recording process.

When we first entered the house, I offered to take Brandon on a tour. He agreed, video camera in hand, and we started on the first floor. The first floor consisted of a study to the right just as you enter the house. A hallway to the left across from the study leads to the parlor room. An embalming table from a mortuary lies in the hallway just before the dining room to the left. The kitchen is the last room at the end of the hall, which also has the door to the basement.

When we got to the second floor I was going into each guest room and talking about the experiences and feelings in each one. The second floor was one big hallway with doors leading into each of the rooms. When I exited the Wedding Suite, I called to Brandon, who was still filming in another room. I looked down at a small couch next to the doorway of the Wedding Suite and saw a small white plate sitting on top of it.

"Did you notice a plate being there?" I asked.

He walked over. "No."

I knew the plate was not on the couch when I entered the Wedding Suite. Brandon filmed the plate and had me recap what happened. The Wedding Suite is basically two rooms with a closet. The first room holds a king-size bed with various windows and furniture around it, including a large mirror next to the bed. The second room of the suite has a small crib with stuffed animals inside of it.

We continued on to the Cora Diehl Suite. I told him about Mike and Karen, who stayed in the room, and the stories about the guests having alleged experiences in there. As we were talking to each other, we heard footsteps going up the staircase to the third-floor attic room. I had yet to see the attic room, so I had no idea there was only one way in and one way out. The entrance door was locked also. We exited the suite, unlocked the attic room door, and proceeded up.

When we reached the third floor, we both took a look around the room and noticed the closet with all of the toys. *This must be where "Augusta" pulls out the toys and scatters them about*, I thought. The third floor was one large open room with windows. There was an area in the center of the room that had furniture and other items laid about. Brandon continued to film, and I stepped away from the closet and started walking to the main window area. Suddenly, I heard something rolling. I looked down to see a small black rubber ball go rolling past my feet and hit the wall in front of me.

"Logan, was that noise you?" Brandon asked.

"A ball just rolled past me, and I didn't touch anything." If the ball had fallen off one of the ledges, it would have bounced, not rolled, and we would have heard it anyway. I picked the ball up, and we examined it closer. As usual, we filmed a recreation and went back down the stairs to lock up the building and leave until later that night.

When night came, most of the remaining members of the Oklahoma City Ghost Club arrived for the investigation (one member, Jerico, would be joining us later). We met up in the study and discussed the plans for the night. We began with a baseline sweep of the building on the first floor, working our way up. Almost immediately, I started getting a strange feeling of someone following us around the house. More specifically, someone following *us* but watching *me*. I constantly found myself looking over my shoulder and around the corner.

When we got to the second floor, the feeling intensified. I found myself in a confusing daze, unable to focus on the sweep. As we walked into the Bordello Room, I walked to the bathroom at the back of the room and stopped. I indeed picked up on the spirit of a young female child on the floor with us. The feeling was sad and uncomfortable. I couldn't move. I forced myself to proceed with the sweep, carrying this overwhelming sadness with me. As we exited the room and proceeded to the next, I felt as if she were grabbing ahold of my leg and I was dragging her down the hall as I walked. The weight was very heavy, and for a moment I wondered if I was having some sort of physical problem with my leg. I had to once again stop and bring myself back into the investigation. Brandon even took notice of my behavior and asked if I was okay. I didn't go into any detail but just told him I was experiencing some things.

When we got into the Wedding Suite, we took note of a few things we thought felt out of place. First, there was a small crib in the second room that was filled with dolls. Earlier as we were filming in the house, the dolls were untouched and sitting normally in the center of the crib. Now the dolls were covered up with a blanket and leaning to the side as if someone or something had tucked them in. We took a few pictures and went back into the main room.

An odd smell manifested in the main room. Some described it as a burnt rubber smell. We then noticed that something was written in a smear on the mirror—Hello. We did not notice it before, and no one had been inside the room. Perhaps the spirit used the smell to get our attention so that we could see the message scrawled across the mirror? We cleaned the mirror and decided to monitor it to see if anything else was written throughout the night. We finished the sweep of the house and made our way downstairs.

We opted to take a break for a while, and I tried to open the first door to exit the house. The door was locked. I knew we had locked the main door of the home, but I was unaware of anyone locking the inside door. I asked the rest of the team about it, and they denied locking the door and were under the assumption that I had locked the door unintentionally. I told them I locked the door leading to the outside and felt there was no cause to lock the inside door. I left the door unlocked and we proceeded to the porch. At this point, Jerico arrived.

With the last investigator at the house to help, we started a second sweep of the inn, but as we were preparing to start, he had battery issues with his flashlight.

The stairs at the Stone Lion Inn.

Even before the sit-down began, we had an unexplainable event. We walked down to the entrance to the third-floor staircase. Brandon and I decided to go inside the Lucille Mulhall Suite for a quick moment when we heard Albert yell, "Logan!"

"What's up?" I asked.

"Where's Brandon?"

"In the room with me."

The rest of our team was outside the room when they heard someone walking up the staircase to the third floor. The door was unlocked, but no one was found inside the upstairs room.

We carried our equipment up to the third floor and set up for the sit-down session. During the experiment, we heard several taps and noises from inside the room that could not be accounted for.

Jerico decided to conduct a knock test, in which he would knock on the floor three times and try to get a response from the spirit. Once he did this, there was one loud solid knock following his three. The room was quiet and still. Suddenly, a few of the team members reported hearing a giggle of a small child and red flashing lights near the toy closet of the room. At first I thought someone might have been using the IR thermometer and was mistaking the laser for an anomaly. This was not the case, as we did not have one currently on the third floor.

I sensed that the child who was in the room was not the same little girl who was following me around. Was this perchance another child spirit of the inn? Did my follower have a sister who also passed when she did? I can't say the spirit was identical to the other, but they were both young.

We finished our sit-down and headed down to the study for a shorter sit-down. As we sat there, nothing of interest happened. There were no anomalous noises or sightings. The sensation I had been feeling was gone as well. *The little girl must have gone to bed,* I thought to myself.

We packed up and headed out the door to the car when we realized the door was locked once again. This was the third time that night we had been locked in. I made the comment that the house did not want us to leave, but I knew the truth: she did not want me to leave.

I never picked up on her name or the name of the other child in the home. Yes, I felt there could be potentially more than one child in the home. Before leaving, I made a short walk down the first-floor hallway and assured her that I would return and that she had nothing to worry about. I locked the doors, returned the keys to Luker's residence, and drove back home.

Final Thoughts on the Stone Lion Inn

Over the years, I have conducted multiple other investigations of the Stone Lion Inn, and with permission I will continue. I have observed everything from doors moving on their own to disembodied voices appearing out of nowhere. I feel that the home is a great place to conduct research due to the never-ending level of activity. Another trip to the Stone Lion Inn will always be warranted, for the home may very well be haunted until the end of time.

The Santa Fe Depot

The Santa Fe Depot is said to be haunted by one of the original Harvey Girls, waitresses of the Southwestern hospitality chain, Harvey House, which often stationed establishments along the railway and grew popular starting at the end of the nineteenth century. The entity that has been picked up both in feeling and in photograph is an elderly woman named Pearl. The abandoned depot has been investigated extensively over the past several years by several paranormal investigation teams, and all have their own conclusive evidence.

First Investigation: The Elevator from Hell

I first got my opportunity to investigate the station back in 2005. It was a joint investigation effort by my paranormal team, of which I was currently the director, and a second team that we worked with. We investigated the mercantile building across the train tracks, the Fairfield building behind the depot building, the depot building itself, and a train car, all abandoned.

In the basement of the mercantile building a strange event happened. As we walked through the dark hallway of the basement, I heard talking. It wasn't like someone was talking in front of me; it was a muffled set of voices. We all stopped to analyze the situation and try to discover where the voices were coming from. We had the two-way radios in our hand, so we knew it wasn't coming from interference on the radios. I then pulled my digital audio recorder from my pocket to learn that not only did it stop recording, but it also began playing the recorded data on its own. I reset it to begin recording again and made my way through the basement and back up.

A bit later, we switched buildings and ended up at the Fairfield building. There were two main floors and a basement, all accessible by a pull-rope elevator. We swept the main floor with equipment looking for activity and then hopped in the elevator and pulled our way into the basement opening. We entered the darkness of the basement and walked around. It was a very small space with a dirt floor. We all experienced an uneasy and uncomfortable feeling of dread. It wasn't long before we all agreed not to stay in the basement any longer. As we made our way up, I looked down and saw something scurry past the opening and move toward the back of the basement. I didn't say anything to the three other investigators as we moved to the top floor; I just kept a close eye on the basement opening.

We made our way up to the top floor, which was a vary large open area, similar to the second floor of a barn. We walked around taking readings and listening for anything unusual. As we completed our sweep of the top floor, we all gathered on the elevator. Now, keep in mind there were four investigators on the elevator, three of whom were significantly bigger than the fourth. There were over nine hundred pounds on that elevator platform. We started to release the brake and make our way down when I felt the bottom of the elevator drop out from under my feet. In a last-second effort to save myself, I jumped off the platform and landed knee-first into the floor. I rolled onto by back and looked back at the elevator to see three heads sticking up just above the landing looking at me. I could see the "What the hell did you do that for?" look in their eyes. I guess the elevator stuck after falling a few feet.

Abandoned on the second floor, we radioed one of the other investigators, who promptly raced into the building with a ladder so we could get down. Once we were safely on ground level, we continued our investigation of the next building, which was the main depot building. We started upstairs and searched through the rooms. There were about three or four rooms in the area above the depot, and one of these was where the spirit of Pearl was captured in a photograph. The rooms were basically used for storage. I did have an unusual feeling of being watched in the room facing the train tracks.

We then came back downstairs and explored the restaurant area and main depot room. The restaurant was one room with tables and other restaurant-related furniture. This restaurant was located between the main depot room and the museum room, where model trains could be found. All the investigators got together and decided to conduct a sit-down in the main depot room. The main depot room was a large open area where I have held conventions in the past. There was a large stage-like platform at the back of the room with tables that could be placed throughout the room. As we were asking questions, we heard noises coming from the upstairs area, including footsteps. When the session was complete, we gathered the equipment and headed home. With an open invitation to conduct more investigations, we felt it would only make sense to return in the near future.

Second Investigation: The Ghost Passenger

The next set of investigations took place as a fundraiser for the depot. In the summer of 2006, we spent four different nights leading the public through several areas of the building to search for paranormal activity. The Santa Fe Depot needed preservation and salvation due to falling behind in finances. We were more than happy to assist by conducting paid tours and donating the proceeds toward saving the depot.

The first one conducted that year was in July, I believe, and very hot. We each took a group of people on a rotation through the separate areas. When my group had their chance to investigate the abandoned train cars something happened. We were sitting in the dining car next to the entryway leading into the kitchen. I was talking with my group about previous experiences and different techniques for investigating. We had equipment set out to measure temperature and EMF.

Suddenly, the door to the dining car slammed right in front of us. I immediately jumped out of the chair and headed for the door. There was no wind present, and the door showed no signs of being manipulated in any way. I tried slamming the door manually several times and could not get it to stay shut. Every time I slammed it, it would bounce back. Under no circumstances could I get the door to slam and catch. We took our seats and started trying to communicate with whoever was on the train with us.

Once we asked if there was anyone there who could communicate with us, we started seeing shadow movement from the back of the first car where we entered.

"Can the person or persons in the car come down to the dining car so we could talk with them some more?" I asked. We then heard glass crunching come from the same car the shadow was seen.

At first it was a loud, obvious sound, and then the crunching grew softer and more silent until it was one pop at a time. All of us felt that someone was waiting for us to come into the first car. I moved closer to the first car and discovered there was a pile of glass on the floor where a window had been busted out. It looked to me like someone was walking on that pile of glass making that noise. This was obvious due to the trail of glass leading to the back of the room and what appeared to be a footprint in the pile of glass. The shadow we saw was on the far back wall. It appeared to be approximately five and a half feet tall with a medium posture. We took about three steps toward the exit and the shadow instantly disappeared. Once we all exited toward the front, we didn't see or hear anything else on the train that night.

Third Investigation: Jumping Shadows
On a separate investigative tour, another set of unusual events occurred in the basement of the depot. One of my tour participants was a fellow paranormal investigator. The basement has two side rooms, one on the right and one on the left. The left room creates a high probability of false positives for EMF due to the circuit breakers and fuse boxes. The right room is a storage area holding various items on shelves and such.

We entered the main area with the group, bypassed the side rooms, and immediately spread out to the back area of the basement. We walked around, and I told the story of the basement and described some experiences investigators have had over the years. While we stood in the back of the room, something was thrown in the right-side room of the basement.

At first I thought something had fallen off the shelf. I walked into the room, and the curious tour members huddled together in the center between the two rooms. Keep in mind that neither of the rooms has doors, so they have two open walkways. Again we heard something suspicious manifest from the right room. I watched closely to make sure that none of the tour members was throwing things into the room. As I was standing guard, I could see in the left room, which was directly across from me. There was a little moonlight that dimly lit the room, exposing the fuse boxes and breakers. I then observed a shadow figure jump in the room and jump back out.

I moved the people standing near the entryway and checked outside to ensure that someone wasn't making the shadows. As I stood in the left doorway, everyone else stood in the right. I then watched the shadow figure of a slouched over image of a person hop in the room and hop back out.

"Can anyone else see the figure?" I asked, and a few said yes. The phenomenon repeated several times, and we then started hearing popping noises start from the back of the basement working their way closer to us. It sounded as if lights were popping out or fuses were being blown. It definitely had an electrical sound to it.

Several members of the tour were taking photographs of the inside of the room. One of them captured a photograph that showed a strange streak of light coming down in a diagonal direction from the wall. The strange thing about the light was that it had multiple colors to it. The top of the light was a yellowish-orange color, while the bottom of the light was a dark blue or purple color. A few members grew uneasy and uncomfortable, so I decided it was time to return to the main area upstairs.

Fourth Investigation: The Basement Entity

When the tours came to an end, I had more time to focus on other areas of the depot, including the mercantile building. Ever since I first went into that basement, I have wanted to go back. A few years ago, I went back with a small group of investigators.

I immediately took the ladder down to the basement. Armed only with a flashlight, I started my journey around the basement. I didn't make ten steps before I heard shuffling coming from behind me. Convinced someone was waiting in the basement to try to scare me, I stopped. I shined my flashlight around the area, which had no hiding places. I waited a few minutes and started my way through the darkness. I went closer to the end of the hallway and I heard an audible voice from about fifteen feet behind me.

"Mmmmmmm," the voice said. The strange thing is I could not distinguish if the voice was male or female. If I were to guess, I would say the voice was female. I proceeded around the corner and someone tapped me on the right shoulder. I turned around really fast and shined my flashlight, only to find no one there. I then heard a loud, heavy object fall right beside me.

"Is anyone there?" I asked.

I heard a "no" echo from down the hall. This time I was convinced someone was down in the basement or had a recorder in the basement helping them stage this set of events. I looked all over the basement but could not find anything to conclude what I was experiencing was a hoax. I climbed up the basement and finished my investigation for the evening.

Final Thoughts on the Santa Fe Depot

As I said before, many investigators have captured evidence in the buildings at the Santa Fe Depot. One investigator has a photograph of what appears to be Pearl in the top window of the living quarters of the depot. Her group has also collected many EVP as well. The mercantile building was at one time a long-term paranormal research site belonging to another paranormal team.

Sadly, the depot has closed its doors to the public and has since shut down.

Logan County Memorial Hospital

You might say I have left the best for last, and I can say without a doubt that the Logan County Memorial Hospital is the most haunted location in Guthrie. In fact, when anyone asks me what the most haunted place I have ever been to is, I always tell them the hospital in Guthrie, Oklahoma. The building was constructed in 1927, but it wasn't until 1948 when the Bernardine Sisters of the Sacred Heart opened the fifty-five-room hospital. The Logan County Hospital Authority acquired it in 1972, and it stayed with them until the hospital closed its doors in 1978 due to a new facility built down the road. The hospital has been abandoned and haunted ever since, and I have had more confirmed and in-your-face experiences in this building than any other. I couldn't tell you how many times I had driven by the building before I walked into it and was almost hypnotized. It was one of the few places I felt drawn into. It was also a turning point in my career as a paranormal investigator.

One night I drove by the hospital with Phillip, and we observed several individuals gathering in the back of the building. We drove up the driveway to see what was going on and introduce ourselves. They informed us that this location was a long-term research project, and if we were interested in an investigation, we needed to send them an email stating such.

We later joined up with Albert and Penny to research the hospital. The first time I checked out the hospital was the night in July I had booked at the Stone Lion Inn, which was right down the street. I met the group at the Santa Fe Depot and followed them to the hospital. Upon arrival, we were taken on a tour of the hospital, from the basement to the fifth and top floor. We made our way back down and were instructed that we could investigate the building if we wished. I did not experience too much that first night we visited the building, but over the next six months I experienced some of the most direct paranormal activity I had experienced in my lifetime.

First Investigation: Hell Hath No Fury Like the Spirit of a Woman Scorned

One night, I arrived at the hospital and asked if they would lock me in the building alone. The team had no problem doing so and went to the convenience store. They said they would be gone about for twenty minutes, so I would have to stay in the building for at least that amount of time. They told me to knock on the door when I wanted out after they returned.

I was armed with only a flashlight and had no equipment to document anything. The entire building is completely void of furniture, with the small exception of items in upstairs rooms.

The basement is completely empty except a small closet area that doubles as a hub for computer equipment that powers a webcam system. The main hallway is very long and very, very dark when no power or lights are on. I entered the basement and heard them lock the door behind me. I reached the main hallway, walked to the stairwell, and proceeded upward. I made my way through all the floors until I reached the top floor and then returned to the fourth floor to spend a little more time there. I walked very slowly down the hallway as I approached the operating room. I stopped right in the entryway.

"If there are any spirits here, can you make yourselves known?" I called out. I heard a very loud bang in the far-right corner in front of me and a scratching sound come from down the hall behind me. I turned around and shined my flashlight down the hall but saw nothing. I stood there in the middle of the hallway in front of the tiled operating room, looking down at the floor and talking to whoever may be listening.

I could not think of what to say, so I simply stated, "I'm not here to disturb anyone. I just wanted to communicate with whoever may be on the floor with me. I don't have anything with me to document you, so whatever you decide to do would be between me and you."

I paused briefly and looked up, only to see the figure of a woman standing against the back wall. Her appearance was very blurry and distorted, but I could see certain details: the long black hair that passed over her shoulders, the white gown, and the blank, almost featureless face. I didn't move, as I didn't know what to do. I wanted to make two things very clear: first, that I could see her standing there, and, second, that I did not mean her any harm or ill will.

"I can see you standing there right now, and I want you to know that I don't have any equipment with me or anything that can harm or bother you," I said. "Is there anything I can do for you?"

The figure lifted her right arm and appeared to be reaching for me. Her slow, almost sliding walk shifted her closer and closer to me as if she wanted to get ahold of me. An overwhelming feeling of apprehensiveness and fear swept over me like a tidal wave. The immediate impression I got was *leave now.*

I said aloud, "I'm sorry if I have bothered you or upset you in any way. I am now going back downstairs and will leave you to your area." I turned around and started a fast-paced walk to the stairwell door. There were two exits to each floor, one on the back side (which was behind me) and one on the front side (which was behind her, and there was no way in hell I was going to pass her to get to the other one). I never once turned around all the way to the door and beyond.

The stairs went down in a square-shaped spiral and were covered with debris and dust. I didn't want to fall going down them, but I didn't want to slow down either. I had to make haste. Once I descended beyond the third floor, I started getting a feeling that someone was right up behind me. I could then hear her breathing on the back of my neck. The air grew extremely cold, and I could hear the sound of her breath with every exhale. She did not physically touch me (thank God) on the way down, but I bowled through the stairwell door entering the basement.

I stood in the middle of the hallway examining the situation. *What am I doing?* I thought. *Here I was, waiting for something like this to happen, and I just … walked away?* I considered going back up to the fourth floor but quickly decided against it. I turned and started my journey to the exit when I heard a female voice say "come here" from around the corner down the other hallway.

That end of the building, which was around the corner, held the autopsy room and morgue of the hospital. I stopped and thought, *Okay, someone came in the building when I was upstairs and now they are trying to scare me.*

"Okay, I'll be right there," I said sarcastically. I took my flashlight and walked the hallway, looking around and asking if anyone was there or if anyone could hear me. I didn't get a response. Then I heard the voice again. This time it was toward the end of the hallway I was going through a minute ago. I headed back into the main hallway and walked down toward the emergency room located at the other end of the building.

"Is anyone there?" I kept asking. The voice called again, from down the hallway of the morgue. I walked up and down the two hallways four or five times and eventually stopped in the middle. I took a deep breath and growled out of annoyance. It was then that I heard a female voice giggle. It was like she knew she was frustrating me. She was playing a game of come-and-look-for-me, and I was tired of playing. I walked to the exit door hearing "come here" repeatedly all the way there. I banged on the door to escape, and an investigator released the lock and opened the door.

I am unaware of the identity of the spirit, though I was told by a psychic that it was a woman who died in childbirth named Pamela or Pam. I had a coworker who stated her father knew not only that the hospital was haunted, but also who the spirit was specifically. I was unable to verify this or where the spirit was said to have died, but I remember his warning: "Stay clear of that room or face her fury."

Second Investigation: More Experimentation and Rain of Rocks

On a separate night, a few more interesting things happened. I had heard about the hospital activity and the research experiments that had gone on over the previous few years. The team was on the fourth floor (yes, the same one I was chased from), and we decided to try something: we brought a standard golf ball and wanted to see if someone would interact with it.

We announced, "We're going to toss this ball down the hallway, and if you could bounce it around or bring it back to us, we would greatly appreciate it." We stood there almost shoulder to shoulder and tossed the golf ball down the dark, vacant hallway. Seconds passed and nothing happened.

"Did you throw it?" Albert asked. Not two seconds passed before the ball flew past us right between our shoulders. The ball never hit the ground; we would have heard it bounce off something if it had. Something caught it in midair and tossed it right back to us.

Rocks also rained down from nowhere on our cars outside the building, and a similar phenomenon occurred inside the building, with the invisible perpetrator using not rocks but glass. I was walking around on the fourth floor with Albert, Penny, and Jerico when I was hit in the back with a small sharp object. I turned back to look, but no one was there. I then examined the floor to search for the object that hit me. A small shard of glass was on the floor next to my foot. I tossed it away and walked on.

A few steps later I was hit again, only this piece bounced off my shoulder and hit the wall. Convinced someone was throwing things, I walked back to check. No one was there. A few rooms later we started hearing taps hit on the windows of rooms. I walked in one of the rooms and saw something fall to the floor. I looked down and found another piece of glass. There was another tap on the window to my right and again another piece of glass on the floor. The three of us gathered into the center of the hallway, listening to the taps from several rooms. Then it stopped. We waited for about five minutes and went back down the hallway.

Third Investigation: More Fear on the Fourth Floor

The next investigation was a short time later. I arrived at the hospital with Chris, a research team member, and we decided to take a seat in the operating room on the fourth floor. The operating room was an open room with a tiled floor where the surgeries took place.

We set up our chairs and took a seat. I had my digital camera ready for pictures and started taking a few out into the hallway. I took one picture and froze when I saw the results. I looked at the display on the camera and saw what appeared to be a little girl's face on the wall in front of me. I still couldn't move. I then heard what seemed to be footsteps going down the hall toward where I saw the shadow woman who chased me away.

"Did you hear anything?" I asked Chris.

"No."

We sat there for a few minutes, and I looked up above his head at the wall and saw a round, green light anomaly zigzag across the wall behind him. It was a solid, green orb.

"I'm going downstairs and outside, and you'll have to be alone for a few minutes," I said. I could tell Chris was uncomfortable and scared to stay up there alone, but I left anyway. Outside, I grabbed some different equipment and told the other investigators about what I had encountered.

They said they were not surprised, as they had seen anomalies like that before in another area. I returned inside to Chris since I didn't know how long he would last alone on an insanely haunted floor. I walked back into the operating room and found him sitting quietly. I asked him if he heard anything strange, but he hadn't. We tried asking questions and hoped for responses, but we were unsuccessful at the time.

We decided to head back downstairs to hit a different area. We met up with the others and started a baseline sweep of the building. I took pictures throughout the various floors of the building. Nothing else interesting happened during the sweep or sit-down.

A ghostly face was captured in the window of a room's door.

When I got home, I started going over my evidence. One picture in particular caught my eye. I zoomed in but didn't see anything I could identify. After I enhanced the image with some color settings, a face appeared in the doorway to one of the hospital rooms. The face seemed to be looking out at something or someone.

Fourth Investigation: The Dark Entity They Call "Mr. Death"

Most of our experiences came during the sit-down sessions, which took place at the end of the investigations. The sit-down sessions usually occurred between two and three in the morning and usually lasted about an hour. Most of the time nothing significant happened, but on one night in particular I saw something happened that I had never seen before.

The local team and I set up a few EMF arrays on both ends of the main hallway of the basement. There was one about four to five feet away from me to my left. During the sit-down, I was watching the array for activations and saw a black shadow mass come out from behind the array, pass in front of it (blocking out the LED pilot light), and go back behind it from the other side.

I quickly yelled to everyone else about what I had seen. They had seen that before and stated that they would make a note of it. I kept a close eye on the mass, and a minute or two later it happened again, only this time I was looking at the shadow on the wall the mass had cast. As it moved around the array, I saw a big figure on the wall as the shadow disappeared. The figure looked almost hunched over with its hands extended out.

One investigator stated that he had seen the shadow pass the pilot light the second time but he didn't see the shadow on the wall. It was rare to see meter activations during a hospital sit-down. Apparently, it's even rarer to experience this shadow phenomenon. I was convinced this was the notorious entity investigators referred to as "Mr. Death" that was seen and felt on the fifth floor of the hospital at times.

Final Thoughts on the Logan County Memorial Hospital

Overall, there are many experiences to have in the abandoned hospital. However, there was not much physical evidence captured over the years. Probably the most compelling is the webcam captures of the woman I encountered on the fourth floor. One of them captured the back of her watching the team walk through the second floor. The other was captured in the basement where you can see her standing next to the team down the hall in the basement. This was an IR capture, but you can still see the details very well. There are still webcams set up to this day—you can log online and watch activity in the old hospital. I don't remember getting any EVP from the hospital. Even though most of the voices you will get will be audible, they do not seem to manifest onto audio. A handful of EVP have been captured over the past eleven years, but it is not a common occurrence. Regardless, there is plenty of paranormal activity to go around. While its activity is not always present, I can say without a doubt that the old hospital is very haunted and probably one of the most haunted places I have ever been and will ever go.

Final Thoughts on Guthrie, Oklahoma

In conclusion, I can say without a doubt that Guthrie is the most haunted town in Oklahoma. There are many more sites in this town that I have investigated that are not included in this chapter, and there are many I have not yet investigated. It is unknown as to why the city is so haunted but it seems everywhere you go in Guthrie, there is a haunted location nearby. I find this area almost sacred because I have had my more memorable experiences there, and I can only hope that one day I will be able to explore them all further.

Chapter 8
THE ABANDONED CHURCH
Rural Oklahoma

This location is probably one of the most intense places I mention in this book. While it is not the most popular or largest haunted site, it is the one of the most threatening and intimidating sites I have ever investigated. Due to some conflicts with an author disclosing information about this building and concerns from the property owner, the name and location of this building must remain a secret. I can only offer the details that surrounded my experiences there.

Little is known about this single-story abandoned building. It sits across from a cemetery hidden in the back roads of rural Western Oklahoma. Very little research can be done on this site, but I have learned it was once an African-American church in the 1950s. I heard about the church through another team that had investigated the site about a year prior to our meeting.

First Investigation: Leave or Die
The problem with setting up an investigation with the site was not that no one *wanted* to go but that no one knew *where* to go.

The team members could not remember how to get there and we couldn't get any of the locals to tell us where it was. A few months later, one of our investigators, Frankie, found the site while on a routine job run in the area. I have to admit I was a bit skeptical at first, but once I learned he was accurate in his discovery, I set up an investigation.

I made my first trip to the church a few days later with investigators Frankie and Ferron to explore the old church. We traveled down the empty dirt road, waiting for the church to appear from out of the darkness ahead. When we arrived, we took the equipment out of the trunk and proceeded into the building. We made our way around the first floor and eventually into the basement. The first floor was one single room with debris all over, from trash to burned out fragments of the building. There was no glass in the windows, so everything was open. Graffiti covered all the walls inside, from satanic words to explicit images. There is a small staircase leading down to the basement area. The basement is very small with small glassless windows looking up to the outside. More graffiti is spread throughout the basement and a small opening in the back leading to the outside of the back of the church.

Our audio recorder was running for EVP, and I took several photographs throughout. While on the chancel, I noticed a dark shadow passing in front of the doorway. I looked outside to see anyone had snuck up and tried to scare us, but no one was outside. We finished our investigation and started back home.

Ferron started listening to the EVP in the car on the way home and made a startling discovery. During the sweep, we walked through the basement entrance at four minutes and thirty seconds into the recording. At that time, a male voice whispered, "You shouldn't be here."

We were still sweeping the basement, and at nine minutes into the recording (exactly four minutes and thirty seconds after the first whisper) and with us in the exact same location, the same voice said, "You shouldn't be here, or you're going to die." While we didn't have too many personal experiences, this EVP alone was enough evidence to warrant another investigation.

Second Investigation:
The Assault of the Basement Entity

A few weeks later I returned to the church with Phillip and investigators Chris, Claudia, Tree, and Christina. The ride up to the church was interesting enough with six people crammed into my car. As we approached the church, my investigators started freaking out on me. Claudia said she had a bad feeling about the investigation and started crying and screaming hysterically. We all got out of the car and headed toward the building when Chris began throwing up. He walked off the church grounds and back to the car. After a moment, he said he was feeling better, so he started back toward the church. Once he stepped back on church grounds, he was throwing up again.

"It's a good idea to stay in the car with Claudia," I told him. Leaving the two of them in my car, the other four of us covered the entire first floor. Two investigators proceeded up to the area around the altar, which left me and Phillip on the main floor. I then heard scuffling from the area of the basement, as if someone were dragging their shoes across the floor, and I could also hear what I perceived to be a low-toned mumbling. I walked toward the entrance to the basement and shined my flashlight down inside. I didn't see anything but continued to hear sounds. I was concerned that, given the church's back-woods location, there might be an animal down there that would attack us.

A minute or so had passed when a large gust of wind—along with something else—came up from the basement and pushed me back with enough force that my feet literally left the ground, and I landed about six feet from where I was standing.

"Phillip, did you see what happened?" I called.

"Yes! Are you okay to continue?" he asked.

Together we headed down to the basement. We walked down to find nothing noticeable inside. We headed back upstairs and continued our walk-through of the first-floor area. I approached one of the broken-out windows and looked across the street at the cemetery. The brightness from the dome light in my car grabbed my attention. I looked over and focused on the inside of the car. *What are they doing in there?* I thought. I then spotted a dark figure peering in the driver's side window at them.

The figure was about as tall as the side mirror on the car and was curiously looking in the window to see what they were doing. I adjusted my eyes and moved my head to make sure I wasn't seeing a shadow from a tree or something else. The figure then turned its head around toward me. It had no eyes or distinct features. Once it made the connection that I could see it, it zoomed away down the road.

Right away, I told Phillip what I had experienced, and we wrapped up the investigation shortly after. We drove down the road away from the church, but Tree and Claudia claimed they felt like whatever was inside the church was following us down the road. Once we passed the first intersection, the feeling was gone. I felt whatever it was just wanted to make sure we were headed in the right direction and not coming back, which is typically what a guardian does. A guardian is a spiritual protector that watches over a location to keep evil spirits and intruders out. There can be good or evil guardians in place over locations.

Third Investigation: Covered in Darkness

After that experience, we returned multiple times to the church for further investigations. On one particular case Brandon was with me. We entered the church and made a walk-through of the building. As we walked, we saw shadows outside, passing the windows and circling the church. I asked Brandon if he could see the phenomenon and he said yes. We decided to stand still for a few minutes to monitor the activity. We leaned against the wall of the main entrance of the church. Other than the soft wind blowing outside, the room was silent. We continued to watch the shadows pass.

Out of nowhere Brandon jumped back and looked down at the floor.

"What happened?"

"Something was tugging on my pant leg!" I could tell he was shaken by it, and he kept looking around. I stood back and watched the altar from where we were standing.

"If there is anyone present, can you make yourself known?" I asked. A strong vibration come over me. It was very heavy and almost paralyzing. I looked up to see a black mass starting to fill the roof of the church and creep in our direction. It was so black and dense that the hole in the roof through which you could usually see the moon was completely covered. I could see through the windows that the shadows were passing ten times faster until the outside light was almost darkened. It was a very negative and very angry feeling. It felt like the walls of hell were closing in on us.

Brandon didn't move. "Is it time to leave?"

Still watching the events unfold, I simply said yes, and away we went.

A strange pink light (above time stamp) was captured on film during an investigation at the church.

Fourth Investigation: Heed the Warning

On a separate occasion, I decided against my better judgment to take a few guests to the church. They were Mike and Karen, the couple I met at the Stone Lion Inn the first time I spent the night there. One of the stories I told them was about the experiences I had at the church, and they seemed genuinely interested. I explained that if they went out, it was at their own risk, and I wouldn't be responsible for anything that happened to them or their property.

They agreed, and we met at a gas station in Guthrie on the night of the investigation. I thought it would be in both our best interests if we took our own vehicles so we could leave whenever we wanted to. They followed me to the church, and I took them on a tour of the structure and told them the accounts of what had happened so far. They expressed an uncomfortable feeling about being there, but at the time I could not concur.

We headed down into the basement, only to hear noises coming from outside as if someone were in the bushes walking around. Again, with this being an abandoned location in the middle of nowhere, it would be easy for someone to sneak up on us. Concerned for the guests, I went outside to check for people, but no one was there. I walked back inside and looked around, immediately taking notice of something through the windows. I could see several shadows outside passing the open windows. The feeling of extreme hostility was setting in.

"It's time to go," I told my guests. I felt there was something waiting for us both inside and out. They didn't want to go just yet, but I told them it would be in our best interests for us to leave. They finally agreed, and we started for the cars. I looked back at the church and saw what looked to me like a figure above the main entrance looking down at us. I hurried in my car and started out the driveway. I looked back to see the couple was taking some time to pull out and leave. I was concerned that they would wait for me to leave and go back into the church. They eventually left and followed me to the gas station in Guthrie.

I had not yet exited my car when the husband came up to my car window. I rolled the window down and asked, "What's wrong?"

"There's something you have to see," he said.

The reason he took so much time leaving was that the moment they started to pull out there was an unseen force throwing things from the back of their SUV. They said the tossing continued down the street until they turned onto the road leading to the highway. It was a bit strange, but it made sense. It was obvious something didn't want us there, as if we were interfering. I could see the tossing as a warning to get the hell away and never come back.

The next detail was perhaps the most threatening. Starting at the driver's side window, there were claw marks in mud that appeared to go down to the bottom of the door. They were not finger marks, but it looked as if something sharp scratched down the window to where the glass meets the door. Not only did they have insufficient time to do this themselves, but I didn't think they would want to risk scratching up their new vehicle just to impress me. Additionally, the door was very warm—not scalding hot, but warmer than I thought it should be.

The claw marks made me think. The figure peering into my car during my previous visit was looking into the driver's side window. Could there have been something in the car the entity wanted? Or was it yet another message to stay away from the church? I saw a connection between the times we had been out there: the entities seemed to pick on or focus on the new people we brought out. If they were not recognized, something always happened.

The question then becomes, who is haunting the church? Most people believe the church is haunted by demons due to the satanic graffiti and rituals that have been said to take place out there. I have yet to find a sacrifice but would not be surprised if I did someday.

Fifth Investigation: Running through the Cemetery

Some of you may be asking, "Has anything else physically attacked you there?" Not that I can remember, but I did go there one time with two other investigators and witnessed more strange phenomena.

I arrived sometime shortly after Memorial Day 2006 with Chris and Jerico. After entering the church and making our sweep, we took a seat near the altar. I sat between the other two investigators, and we focused our attention on the main entryway of the church. We heard a few sounds as we were walking around, and most of them were generated near the front doorway.

It wasn't long before I was hit in the back with a rock. I turned around to see if there was anyone in the direction of where the rock came from. At first I thought it could have fallen from the ceiling, but the rock came at me horizontally, not in a falling motion. There was an open area behind us where a window once was, so I thought someone could have been hiding outside. I quickly verified there was not anyone around and continued the sit-down.

A strange light appeared in the corner of the room. The light was small and round, about the diameter of a quarter, and was very dim. It appeared for about five seconds and just disappeared. We could not get any responses after several attempts at communication.

I suddenly got the feeling that we were in the wrong place. I knew we had to go across the street to the cemetery. Before this night, we really had not gotten any significant data from the cemetery, but we decided to check it out anyway.

We entered the cemetery from the main gate and started toward the back. As we walked, we noticed a small black form near one of the back headstones and a tree. At first glance I thought it was a dog. I told Jerico, who was a few steps ahead of us, to watch out for the wild animal ahead. He looked and confirmed the shadow.

He then started running toward it at full speed. Several of the graves had plastic American flags and other military decorations for Memorial Day on them. As Jerico ran past, each one snapped as if someone had broken it in half. Once he got near the grave, the shadow darted straight up the nearby tree. We did not move until we witnessed the form take flight.

I was compelled to attend to Jerico but also to check the flags that snapped.

"Are you okay?" I asked him, and he confirmed he was. I shined my flashlight down at each grave, inspecting the flags. None of them were damaged or moved.

Chris was preoccupied looking for the form behind nearby gravestones. The three of us walked through the cemetery toward the main gate. I shined my flashlight around at the other headstones and noticed it started to flicker as if it were going to go out. I felt a small breeze blow past me very gently, which I thought was odd since there was zero wind that night. I turned around and did not see anything.

As I looked all the way up the tree next to me, the light on my flashlight started going out; when I looked at the branches, the light died. I found myself looking directly at the black form that was taunting us. I took a huge step back into one of my investigators. I never took my eyes off the form, and as I backed up, it flew out of the tree and directly across to another tree.

After a few seconds, it shot straight up into the night and disappeared. The sound was very loud and the tree shook.

"What's going on?" the others inquired. They thought a flock of birds had flown out of the tree. I explained what was going on, and we again searched the ground and sky for the form.

We did not see or hear anything else that night related to the previous events. We packed up and headed home.

Final Thoughts on the Abandoned Church

I have been back to the church a handful of times after the last major incident and about fifty times in total over the past eight years. At times, it appeared that there was something there, but human threats were the major concern. While most of the church's regulars are kids partying and drinking, I feel there are other problems present at times. I don't know if some people are going out there conjuring up spirits or if there is other reasoning behind what we feel while we are there. I do know that the place is not safe at times. One of the other threats out here is wild animals. Coyotes and mountain lions are the biggest local sightings. Sometimes there is nothing at all out there and it is very quiet. However, it is not worth the risk of your safety or your life.

I also urge all readers not to attempt to find this location. The owners of the property do not want anyone there and will call the police if they detect any visitors. It is not worth going to jail or getting killed. I can't say I won't ever go back to the abandoned church, but I don't know when I will return either. I don't know if the building is active anymore because I haven't been there in quite a while, but I do know that in the past the building and its dark occupants loved to raise hell.

Chapter 9
THE KITCHEN LAKE BRIDGE
Oklahoma City, Oklahoma

In every city in the country, there are areas with urban legends and local folklore about being haunted by spirits. Most deal with a "Crybaby Bridge" or haunted train tracks where someone died in a car accident. There is such a location hidden away in the back areas of Oklahoma City, a small lake to the east called Kitchen Lake. The road passing this lake leads down to an area where a bridge connecting two roads is now destroyed, leaving only a small portion of the bridge. The road is blocked off from traffic, but you can easily walk on foot to the area. I had heard several stories involving the area in regard to paranormal activity and people that had experiences out there. The site was a well-known party site for the young kids out drinking and looking for a place to go scare themselves. It was also a dumping ground for unwanted furniture.

The story about the origin of the "curse" of Kitchen Lake begins with a woman who lived in a small house about a mile down the road from the bridge. This woman was said to have practiced ritual magic and was labeled as a witch by the locals.

She had a son who was around the age of five. One day, the child left the house and wandered down to the lake. Somehow, he ended up in the lake and drowned.

A sign for Kitchen Lake.

I have heard two different versions of the ending to this story. One was that the woman was overwhelmed with grief and secluded herself in the house. One day, her depression got the best of her. She locked herself in the home and set the house on fire, drowning away her sorrow in a gulf of suicidal flames. The second ending to the story was that she met her demise at the hands of a group of locals. Apparently, after learning of her child's death, the locals thought that she had killed her son in some sort of sacrifice to the devil. They waited until they knew she was home and barricaded her inside so that she could not escape. They then set the home on fire and watched it burn, hearing only her screams from inside as it was destroyed.

Despite these stories, I was not overly convinced that this area was haunted. It was the eyewitness accounts of the events taking place out there that made me want to see for myself. I spoke with a woman who claimed she was out at the site late one night with some friends. They had heard the story from someone at a local convenience store and decided to go investigate. When they arrived, they got out of the car and started walking around the area. They noticed that up the road leading to the bridge there was a person kneeling on the ground and doing something to the fence. They had assumed it was a homeless person because she wore old dirty clothes and had long dirty hair. One of the party called out to her, and she turned around to face the party.

She had bright blue, almost white, eyes, and her face was covered in dirt or mud. She briefly lunged at the party before scurrying back toward the area of the bridge. One of the members of the investigative party ran after her but said she disappeared when he reached the bridge itself. They did not stay at the site long before heading out back into the city.

First Investigation: The Glowing Fires of Hell

After hearing this story, I felt the site would be a good one to check out. I asked Phillip if he would be interested in joining me, and he agreed. In late 2004, we made our first trip to the Kitchen Lake Bridge with Rachel and Rita (two newbie investigators). We took Phillip's truck and made our way to the convenience store down the street from the lake.

Phillip felt it was best that we make a plan for what to do once we arrived on site. Not having been to the site before, we felt our first trip should be quick, so Phillip and I rode in the cab of the truck while two other investigators were in the bed of the truck. Rita had a camera to take pictures of the area.

We made our way to the road leading to the bridge. We stopped briefly at the remains of the house the woman lived in but decided we would come back when we returned from the bridge. We continued down the road until we could not drive any further. A Bridge Out sign was blocking our path as well as three large rocks that lay stacked in the middle of the road. We kept the truck running and the headlights shining on the sign, but the reflection from the sign was almost blinding to us.

The two investigators in the back started taking pictures of the area, including the area in front of us. Meanwhile, Phillip and I both noticed a very sickening smell entering the cab of the truck. All the windows were up, so I knew it wasn't coming in from outside.

We looked at each other. "Do you smell that foul odor?" we asked each other. Almost immediately, the truck started stalling out and the headlights began to dim. Phillip said that he thought it was a good time to leave and started backing up to turn the truck around so we could drive out, seeing that there was only one way out of there. As he was turning the truck around, the grass started moving by a fence across from us. The movement traveled through the grass toward the truck as if someone were moving in our direction. Phillip finally got the car turned around and we took off toward the location of the witch's house.

When we pulled up to the location of the house, we found that we needed to climb over barbed wire to get to it. I say "house," but actually all that was left was the foundation and the chimney. One of the eyewitness reports indicated that at times, there would be smoke and fire coming from inside the chimney. When people would investigate, there was nothing in the chimney to indicate that anything was burned—no burning smell or ash. I could easily see how someone could have gotten to the foundation to start the fire only to return and clean up afterward. I knew the story was probably not paranormal, but I wanted to investigate it regardless. We walked over to the chimney and sat down on the foundation. We ran some audio very briefly but felt the wind and other outside elements would be too much contamination. After about ten minutes of walking around and dodging random patches of cow manure, we decided to get back into the truck and head home.

The next day I dropped off the film at the local pharmacy (this was before I converted to digital cameras) and waited the hour for the film to process. I had to remember to tell the technician to make sure and keep all the photographs so that they would not discard one after seeing an anomaly and thinking it was a defect in the film. Back at home, I took the photos out and noticed something in the very first picture. It was a picture of the three large rocks and Bridge Out sign at the end of the road by the bridge. I noticed an eerie red glow coming from the middle pile of rocks and a small red particle that appeared to be floating away from the rocks like embers of a fire.

Another thing was the Bridge Out sign. When we first saw the sign, it looked almost new. I didn't see a scratch or mark anywhere on it (and I had a very good look with the headlights shining directly on it). However, in the photograph, the sign was severely damaged and graffiti was covering a good part of it. In some areas, the sign was broken and moved tilted away from the rocks.

I immediately called Phillip to ask him about the sign.

"Do you remember the Bridge Out sign?" I asked.

"I do," he said.

"Do you remember the condition of the sign?"

"Yes, it was in good condition."

"I got the photographs back and want to show you them in person to get your opinion."

I met up with him at a local restaurant and showed him the picture. He could not believe either of the unexplained images in the photograph. Both of us agreed that it warranted another visit to the Kitchen Lake Bridge, so with that we finished our meal and made our way back to the location.

Second Investigation: A Walk in the Woods

Our second trip started around nine, just after recruiting Frankie and Rachel to go with us. Phillip and I decided to explore the area more this time and try to gather more evidence. We started at the old bridge where we took the pictures. This area was rumored to be cursed by the witch. According to the stories, she used to steal the belongings of the locals and anyone who dared enter that area. She would pile these belongings in small circles and burn them as a part of a cursing ritual.

We got out of the car and first looked at the Bridge Out sign. It looked exactly like it did in the photograph, even though everyone who was there said it looked well-kept on the first visit. We also looked at the rocks. There was no evidence of any fire or that anything had been burned there recently. We ventured past the road into the woods, where the bridge was. The only thing left of the bridge was steel beams that connected the two areas. It was possible to make it from one side to the other but very dangerous. The safest way was to climb down to the small creek, cross, and make your way back up the other side. We took a few pictures of the bridge and surrounding area and then made our way back to the rocks.

Rachel and I decided to try some EVP sessions. I walked over to the fence and placed the recorder down on the ground. I knelt and started asking questions.

"If anyone is out there, can you come to where I am and talk to me?" I asked. "Follow my voice."

The tall grass about twenty feet away on the other side of the fence began to move. It was moving from left to right, and we could hear rustling on the ground. With this being a field, I figured it was an animal of some sort. I just hoped it was nothing that would threaten us or something that would cause us misery during our investigation. I kept talking to whoever might have been around us and noticed that the movement in the tall grass was headed our direction. Rachel and I took a step back and waited for whatever it was to come out of the grass and into the open area between us and the fence. We kept hearing the rustling but noticed the tall grass stopped moving. I then looked to the ground and noticed small indentions moving toward our location. I knelt back down and lowered my voice to a softer tone so I wouldn't frighten it away. The footsteps got to about five feet from us before they stopped. I pleaded with it to say something to the recorder so we could hear its voice.

Suddenly, Phillip yelled something. Whoever or whatever it was rushed off back into the woods, leaving the two of us there feeling like someone just ruined Christmas.

We decided to head back to the foundation of the house. The four of us climbed over the fence and approached the chimney. It was a very cold, dark, and quiet evening. We sat on the edge of the foundation and started taking pictures. I walked to a tree to see if I could capture some anomalies in photographs. I briefly looked back toward the foundation and saw Phillip and the other two investigators running toward me like a stampeding herd of buffalo.

"Run!" yelled Phillip, hauling ass to get back to the car. Not knowing what was going on, I frantically raced with them. I tried leaping over the barbed-wire fence, only to get it stuck between my legs just a quarter inch from causing an unfortunate injury. I pulled myself over just in time to see Phillip do a Superman jump, leaping with his arms straight forward into the back seat of the car. Once we were all in the car with the doors locked, I had to inquire about what was going on.

Phillip explained, "As we were walking though the field toward the tree line, we noticed a truck idling at the stop sign. We were worried the driver was watching us, thinking we were going to steal a cow." Then someone had said "shotgun!" and everyone hysterically started running for the car for their lives.

Once calm and serenity overcame us again, we decided to give up the investigation for the evening and head back home.

Third Investigation: The Firefly

I took a coworker to the site late one night. We made it to the foundation with no issues and got out of the vehicles. I started telling the stories of the woman who lived in the house and the legends of her death. We safely crossed the fence and walked to the foundation. While we sat on the foundation and took note of the tree line leading into the woods, the notion that someone could try and sneak up on us for an ambush was in the back of my mind.

As I was watching the trees, I noticed a small, round light appear from the left-hand side of the tree line. It floated along the trees and quickly disappeared. *A firefly*, I thought.

Nothing special, right? It seemed that way at first...

Fourth Investigation: The Witch Takes Form

On a separate investigation, I caught one of the most compelling photographs of my tenure investigating in the paranormal. This time, however, I was equipped with a digital camera for instant results. It was particularly cold this evening, and Phillip and I were wearing winter coats. We were alone for this trip but felt safe because Phillip was there. He was a survivalist, somewhat of a MacGyver. I knew if we ever backed into a corner, Phillip would make a weapon out of a pile of leaves and twigs to take down our enemy.

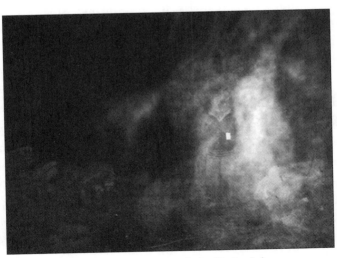

The angelic form photographed at Kitchen Lake.

We started walking the grounds, taking pictures along the way. I got one picture that had a bizarre light anomaly in it: there was what appeared to be an angelic form. I also captured another photograph of a strange light anomaly forming what appeared to be a cross. Some may find it more than coincidence that a cross and an angel were captured in two separate photographs on the same night. But neither of these would top what I captured next.

As we were walking down toward the bridge, Phillip suddenly stopped. "Logan, will you start taking pictures?"

"Why?"

"I feel something in front of me that's watching me ..."

With that said, I started taking pictures of him from a short distance. To my disbelief, one of the photographs caught something I had never seen before. On the right side of the picture you see Phillip, and on the left you see standing over him a seven-foot-tall smoky form that was almost human looking. The form had both its arms extended out like it was going to grab him. I could even make out what appeared to be a face and large nose as well as, again to my disbelief, a pointy hat on top of the head.

Now, I would find this hard to believe if I were anyone else, and I can't say without a shadow of doubt that this was a manifestation of something paranormal, but it is very hard to discount given the fact that Phillip specifically said he felt something in front of him and watching him. After taking the photograph, I inquired about this "feeling" he was experiencing. He said it was like a static-electrical feeling was pulsating through the front of his body. I noted the experience and we continued.

We made our way to the bridge, climbed down to cross the small creek, and then climbed up the other side. I began taking photographs as Phillip started asking questions for EVP. As

I was snapping pictures, I noticed in one of the photographs that there was a strange form coming from the other side of the bridge. The form was distant and appeared to be someone standing in the background, only it was more of a shadow figure than an image of a person. I told Phillip that I thought someone was back toward the car and that we should head that way because I didn't want to risk someone breaking into the car. We crossed over again and headed toward the vehicle, only to find no one there. We made a few more attempts to communicate with someone who could be there and then packed up and headed home.

Fifth Investigation:
The Ring of Fire and Dancing Lights

Over the next year, I made several more visits to the bridge, this time with my friend and former colleague Brandon. Brandon took an interest in the case after I had told him of the experiences there in addition to some local legends.

One night we found ourselves with nothing going on and decided to make the trip out to the bridge. It was just the two of us, and we had little equipment with us. He basically wanted to see what the site looked like and possibly find out if something would happen when we showed up. I decided to bypass the foundation and go straight to the bridge.

We arrived at the bridge and got out of the car, immediately noticing the smell of something burning. Having heard the story of the witch and her habit of burning items from unsuspecting victims, Brandon was a little uneasy. We noticed some glowing toward the fence line and decided to investigate. When we got to the fence, we saw a circular burn pattern behind the fence. The burn had intersected the fence and actually burned the fence post. There were burning embers from the fence, and it was still smoking. What was so interesting about this was the fact that it looked like a controlled burn. It was a perfect circle burn pattern, but it crossed the fence and reached the road. Both of us agreed that if someone were out there burning land or anything else, we should leave, regardless if it were a witch or not doing the burning.

We drove down the road to the house and crossed the fence. Brandon wanted to see this area because he felt it could possibly be the source of the activity. We sat on the foundation, and I told him about what had gone on while we were there in the past.

Suddenly, in the tree line across the field, we noticed something very interesting. Multiple lights came from the trees. This time they had a blueish tint to them, and they zipped in and out of the trees very quickly. Some of them flew around in a circle together, floated apart, came back together, and then flew off into the trees again. It was very fascinating to watch, and this went on for about fifteen minutes or so before they disappeared and never came back.

Final Thoughts on the Kitchen Lake Bridge

I want to stress to everyone reading this book that this place is not safe. The area has since been roped off, and you can no longer drive down to where the bridge is out. The house's foundation is still accessible from the road, but I would not suggest going there because the chimney has since been knocked down, and there is not much left there from the house that once stood. A friend of Cathy's investigated this place some years ago. She attempted to cross the bridge, slipped, and fell to the creek below. Emergency medical services recovered her from the creek and then rushed her to the hospital. This person is now permanently paralyzed from the neck down because of what happened—not because of a paranormal event or malicious specter, but because of carelessness and doing something that is extremely dangerous. I had many good experiences here early in my career in paranormal investigation and gathered much evidence, but this place is one that I am glad to lay to rest forever.

Chapter 10
THE COUNTY LINE
RESTAURANT
Oklahoma City, Oklahoma

At one time the County Line Barbeque restaurant was a hot spot in Oklahoma City for delicious barbeque. But it wasn't the barbeque, the homemade bread, nor the friendly and courteous staff that brought me through the doors of the County Line. It was the large number of reports of ghostly activity that had been experienced for decades.

In the 1930s the County Line restaurant was known as the Kentucky Club. It is rumored that during this time, the Kentucky Club was a speakeasy parlor with gambling, drinking, and prostitution. There was a story of a man known as "Russell" (or just "the cowboy" by others) who lost his life in the Kentucky Club. In this case as well, two different stories surfaced about how Russell met his maker.

As the first story goes, Russell was a frequent patron of the club, and he met a woman there with whom he started having an affair. Russell was an unmarried man who fell deeply in love with the woman and tried to persuade her to leave her husband

and run away with him. She eventually agreed and left her husband a note that she was leaving him for another man whom she was madly in love with. The woman agreed to meet Russell at the club, where they would make travel plans and initiate their getaway. The husband, who found the letter earlier than the wife had anticipated, intercepted them at the Kentucky Club. There was a brawl between Russell and the husband, and Russell was shot and fatally wounded. The husband grabbed his wife and left the club, never to return. Russell died shortly after being shot. The husband also shot his wife and buried her in an unmarked grave at an unknown location. Eventually caught, he confessed to the crime and was hung for his punishment.

The second story about Russell's death is a little different. In this version, Russell again was a frequent patron of the club. He had habitual flings with many of the prostitutes of the establishment. He favored one woman in particular and met with her quite frequently. Russell was married, and his wife eventually found out about his indiscretions. One night she waited for her husband to leave the house and followed him to the club. She eagerly waited in the shadows to monitor her husband's devious actions. Before long, Russell's favorite showed up and sat on his lap in the main bar area. The wife appeared from the ominous darkness of the corner and shot her husband point-blank twice, knocking him over. He died immediately after being shot. She left the building and went home, only to turn the gun on herself and commit suicide.

In both stories, Russell died right in front of the fireplace in the back area of the restaurant, and this is the area he was said to haunt. Many guests who have dined in that area or sat near it have witnessed numerous unexplainable events, such as plates being knocked over for no apparent reason.

Russell was not the only ghost to haunt the County Line restaurant. There were rumors of a little girl who haunted the basement area, and one of the speakeasy's prostitutes was said to have died there, haunting the area as well. With all this information, I felt it was time to walk through the doors of the County Line myself.

First Investigation: "Stay Out!"

When we first began investigating this location, we were also investigating the hotel next door. There were reports of unexplained fires in the hotel that had more than once caused damage to the building, yet the fire inspectors could find no rational explanation for the cause. On one such investigation of the hotel, I learned some information that might offer some explanation about why the County Line is also haunted.

I pulled up at the hotel and parked the car. Phillip, Rachel, Frankie, and I and started toward the main area of the hotel. Usually, we would wave at the night clerk to let her know we were there, and she would wave back, signaling that she knew we were on-site and would be investigating. This night, the clerk waved for me to come to the desk. I was worried she was going to tell me we could no longer investigate the hotel and had to leave, but this was not the case. I approached the window apprehensively.

"Is everything okay? Is there a problem with us coming out?" I asked.

"Everything's fine," she assured me. "You're good to go, but I want to share some information with you. I did some research, and back in the twenties and thirties, this whole area was patrolled by the mob. When they had people they wanted to punish or make 'disappear,' they would take them to various areas and shoot them, and then bury them somewhere in the area."

I'm not saying any of this is true or that it explains the hotel hauntings or the ones at the County Line, but it would make sense that people who lost their lives so violently and were thrown in a hole in the ground to be forgotten perhaps might be trying to reach out to the living to communicate.

When planning this first trip to the County Line, I had made contact with Brenda, who was the manager at the time. She seemed willing to have me come out and said there were many stories involving "ghosts" and the restaurant. When the team arrived, she promptly seated us at one of the tables in one of the many rooms. She then introduced me to Oscar, a long-time worker at the restaurant who shared many experiences of his own as well as stories about the other employees that had experiences as well. We spoke briefly with Oscar and patiently waited for the restaurant to close.

02/25/2005 09:36 pm

The basement of the County Line restaurant.

The basement of the County Line restaurant.

We decided to focus our investigation in three areas: the up-stairs room, the basement, and the dining area by the fireplace. We started our investigation in the basement, which is one of the areas where the little girl was said to hide out. Setting our audio recorders on the wall, we entered the crawl space under the restaurant. As I began taking pictures of the back of the crawl space, I noticed a strange blue glow in my display on the back of the camera. I took a picture, but the light was not cap-tured in the picture; it only showed up in the display screen on the camera.

Not having enough evidence to conclude it was anything more than strange, I started photographing on the other side of the basement when something hit the back of my left arm. It was small and just heavy enough for me to feel it hit me, but I couldn't figure out what it was. There were three other people in the basement with me, and one of them could easily be trying to make me think that something was being thrown. I walked around by the main door leading to the outside and took a few photographs in the adjoining room. As I was walking out, I could clearly see the other three individuals at the back of the basement setting up something on the wall of the crawl space. I started toward them when I felt something hit my left arm again. This time I looked down to see a small piece of gravel bounce off the floor. The piece came from the direction of the back area, where the air-conditioning equipment was, which was too far to the left of my team's location. I knew it could not have been them. I started taking photographs in the area but was unsuccessful in capturing anything paranormal.

The upstairs room of the County Line restaurant.

We left the basement and returned to the inside of the building. Phillip and I decided to go upstairs while the other two stayed in the main dining area. There were toys left in the upstairs room for the little girl who is said to play in the building. We entered the room and set our audio recorder on the table. I began taking pictures in the direction of the stairs leading back down to the restaurant. Phillip was standing in front of me, and I took a picture. In the photograph I saw a long, white mist-like anomaly behind him. Upon first looking at the picture, one might think it was smoke, yet neither of us were smoking at the time the photograph as taken. I kept snapping pictures to try to re-create the image or possibly get more anomalous photographs but had no success. Phillip and I both returned to the main dining area to continue the investigation.

I took a break for a few minutes, grabbing something to drink and sitting down at one of the tables. Phillip was going through our equipment and asking what we should use during our investigation of the dining area. We decided to run audio and take pictures as well as perform an EMF sweep of the room. At that point we were getting tired and felt like we didn't have much time left, as the employees were wrapping up the closure of the restaurant.

When my break was over, I got up and started taking photographs. I took one picture of the fireplace, where Russell supposedly perished, that came out with a large, round yellowish flare. I showed Phillip the picture, and he immediately began sweeping the area for EMF. To the left of the fireplace he got a small spike. Once he went back to that same spot, it was gone. Then he got a spike about five feet in front of the fireplace; again, he went back and but it was gone. He did this several times as if whatever it was, was moving to different locations at various times. Once all the EMF spikes had disappeared and we no longer were getting readings, he sat down to do some

EVP. He asked the basic questions: "What is your name?" and "Why are you here?" and so on. After about ten more minutes of recording, we decided to call it a night, as the manager was ready to go home.

Once we returned home, Phillip went over the EVP. The next day I met him at his house to review what we may have caught. This time he did not tell me over the phone what voices were captured.

The first EVP was when Phillip asked, "What is your name?" A deep voice said, "Russell."

The second came, not as a response to a question, but as an eerie voice in the background. There was about twenty seconds of silence, and then a voice said, "Why do I sway? Bullet."

The third EVP was of a male voice in response to Phillip asking what we could do to help. The sinister male voice replied, "Stay out!" I felt this was compelling evidence from just our first investigation of the restaurant, so I called Brenda and scheduled a second investigation for the following weekend.

Second Investigation: The Face in the Light

The second investigation started much like the first, only this time we arrived early enough to eat before investigating. It would be Phillip, Rachel, and I returning to the restaurant. We had a new member, Ferron, along for this one, and it would prove to be an exciting first investigation for him in the County Line.

We finished the meal and waited for the restaurant to close. I took the new guy around and showed him the different locations where activity had been reported. We all went down to the basement together and took some readings first so that we would not generate our own false positives. After, we split up, and Phillip and Rachel went back to the restaurant to investigate the second floor.

Ferron and I stayed down in the basement alone. Phillip left a two-way radio for us to stay in contact with each other if necessary. As we sat there on the ground comprising mostly gravel rock, the new guy began telling me about himself, his experiences, and his overall interest in the paranormal. It wasn't long before we starting hearing clicking sounds coming from the equipment in the room: it was a quick eerie click over and over on six instances. Seconds later, we noticed a dim red light appear at the top of the room around the equipment. I didn't worry too much at that time because I assumed the clicking and the light were a result of the equipment turning on.

We began to focus more and more on the red light, and a blue mass began to manifest within the red light. At first it was very small in diameter, probably about the size of a tennis ball. It then grew to about the size of a cantaloupe. Features became more distinct within the blue mass, and we soon realized that a face was emerging out of the light. The eyes appeared along with a nose and mouth. It grew so detailed that we could both see what appeared to be a beard form around the mouth. Both of us were asking each other what the other was seeing, and I think the mutual confirmation made both of us uneasy.

The "head" started moving, very slowly, from left to right, back and forth. I started asking questions about whatever or whoever was trying to appear before us. I had an audio recorder going at the time, so if it responded, I would capture whatever it said.

I asked, "Why are you down here?" Suddenly, the face stopped moving and was completely still. Instead of floating from left to right, it started floating toward us. We started slowly leaning back until our backs were almost against the gravel floor. We were sitting there, paralyzed against each other like two teenagers at a drive-in horror movie. The anomaly got about three feet from us before a loud squelch came over the radio.

"What's going on down there?" Phillip's voice echoed like the voice of God from the heavens above. The face and the red light suddenly faded away, and we were left in complete darkness once again. Needless to say, we turned on our flashlights, gathered our equipment, and raced out the door and back up into the restaurant.

A photograph taken at the
County Line Restaurant during an investigation.

We met up with Phillip and explained what had happened in the basement. Anxious to head downstairs, Phillip gathered up all the equipment and the team and headed to the basement. I did not feel like going back after everything that went on. I was quite shocked that the new guy went back down after what happened, but Phillip can be very persuasive in getting people to investigate. I just wanted to rest, so I took a seat by the fireplace and let them have at it.

About thirty minutes later the team returned. They reported that they got a positive response to a knock test, in which something knocked back at them when prompted. They also reported an apprehensive feeling in the basement but witnessed no visual or sound anomalies aside from the knocking. By that time, it was getting late and the manager was ready to go home, so we packed up and headed out.

A stairway in the County Line Restaurant.

Third Investigation: Anthony Liggits

Over a year passed, and I returned with different investigators. Albert, Penny, Brandon, Jerico, and I would be present for this investigation. They had never had a chance to investigate the restaurant and were excited to have the opportunity.

I walked them around and gave them the tour of the place, noting where we would be investigating. We left our equipment in the main dining area and prepared to head down to the basement. Three employees asked if they could join us because they had never been down to the basement before but heard of the experiences there. I didn't see an issue with it, so I invited them along.

I was at the front of the line walking down the stairs. We reached the door, and the manager was preparing to unlock it when we heard a female voice yell, "Stop!" We all turned around to check if one of the female employees at the end of the line had turned around looking for something or someone. The puzzled look in her face turned fearful after she learned there was no one behind her and the closest person to her was four feet in front of her.

I stopped to asked her, "Are you okay? Why did you scream?"

"As I came down the stairs and turned to head to the basement, someone grabbed the back of my left arm by my elbow. I thought it was another employee and screamed for them to stop," she explained. When she realized no one else was there, she politely requested to be escorted back inside the restaurant.

After the tour, we began our investigation in the basement. Having more equipment than previous visits, I felt I was at an advantage for capturing evidence. We all took our positions and turned out the lights. We started asking questions and telling whoever was there to make a sound so we would know they were present. Before long, we heard small sounds of something being dropped on the gravel. I remember hearing the sound before, as it was the sound that was made when the gravel was thrown at me hit the ground in an earlier investigation.

"Is anyone being assaulted by the gravel?" I asked the team. I got some confused silence. "The strange sound we're hearing is the rocks hitting the floor."

The sounds we picked up almost sounded like rain sprinkling along the ground. We turned on the light and verified that we could not see any rocks moving nor anything else hitting the ground. Soon after, the sounds stopped. It was one of the craziest sound anomalies that I had witnessed in person. We got a few EMF spikes along the wall of the crawl space, but they were short lived and did not manifest any more that night.

Reviewing our evidence, we found we had captured some of the "rocks" sound anomaly, but the sounds were very faint. We also captured us commenting on it. The most impressive EVP we got that night was when the employee was touched outside the door of the basement. After she realized there was no one there and asked to go up to the restaurant, a clear male voice said, "Anthony Liggits." We are unsure if this was the name of the person speaking to us or if perhaps it was someone else telling us who had touched her. Whichever the case, we felt it was an impressive piece of evidence.

Final Thoughts on the County Line Restaurant

I made several other trips back to the County Line restaurant a few years later. Sadly, the County Line Barbecue closed its doors permanently and went out of business. Today, Gabriella's Italian Grill and Pizzeria inhabits the old County Line building, and they too speak of unexplained occurrences going on. They showed me a video of a glass that had pushed itself off the counter for no apparent reason. I believe this location still has many things to offer the study of the paranormal, and I will find myself going back in the future—not only for the ghosts, but for the awesome Italian food as well.

Chapter 11
ARAPAHO CEMETERY
Arapaho, Oklahoma

Everyone who has gone ghost hunting at one point in their life has investigated a cemetery. But few have investigated a cemetery quite like this one. Most people think cemeteries are hot spots for ghosts and paranormal activity because they are literally surrounded by the dead, but this does not necessarily mean they are haunted. Sometimes the land where the cemetery is located is haunted, as some have been known to be on Native American burial grounds and sacred land.

It wasn't the land that brought me to Arapaho Cemetery. It was its notorious reputation for being haunted—by one person in particular.

In 1936 a young woman named Robina Smith died instantly in a car accident with a creamery truck. Her father, George, had long worried about the soul of his long-lost daughter, as he felt she had not been saved by the acceptance of God. Many claim that if you go to Robina's grave late at night, you can hear the voice of her father proclaiming, "Oh Lord, Robina has not been saved!" But it's Robina herself who has been spotted roaming the cemetery late at night, sneaking around and hiding behind the tombstones. When I heard the story, I was skeptical, but I headed out to learn that there was much more behind this cemetery than just stories.

Robina Smith's gravestone in the Arapaho Cemetery.

First Investigation: The Ghost Dog

The first time I stepped foot in Arapaho Cemetery was in November 2003. The place was not easy to find, as it was over an hour and a half from Oklahoma City, and this was before the days of convenient GPS devices (or at least I didn't have one). I made the drive with my friend Tree and my ex Krystal. After a few turnarounds, we finally found the main gate to the cemetery. We drove through and pulled in about fifty to a hundred feet.

It was dark, and we had no idea where Robina's grave was. We all got out of the car to stretch and walk around. The cemetery is on a hill with a circular drive around the cemetery. Many headstones and trees are laid throughout the cemetery, making it impossible to locate one grave in particular without close investigation. Tree and I walked around the immediate area to look for Robina's headstone, but we were unsuccessful.

"Let's drive farther to the back of the cemetery, where we can access more headstones," I suggested. We packed back into Tree's car, only to find it would not start. The car was not turning over nor making a noise of any kind. I was a little worried about being in the cemetery after dark in the middle of nowhere with no one to help us. Tree popped the hood of his car to see if he could visibly figure out what the problem was. He saw nothing that he could identify, so he left the hood up and walked back to the car.

I could see that he was getting worried, and with it being November, the weather was getting colder. I finally gave up and decided to call AAA for a wrecker, but the representative said it would be one and a half to two hours before someone could get to us. What choice did we have? I told him we would be waiting for his call or for someone to show up.

When I hung up the phone, I noticed it had gotten increasingly darker since we first arrived. It was eerily silent with no noises other than a pump jack for oil that was running in the distance. We chatted with each other, and the wind started to pick up. It was getting louder, howling almost—very unsettling for the current situation. Not having a weapon to protect ourselves was even more unsettling, but I don't think a gun would have saved us from anything supernatural.

I got back into the car's driver seat and closed the door. I laid my head back and closed my eyes, only to feel like I was moving. I opened my eyes, and the car was moving forward.

But how could that be? It wasn't even on. I looked down to the gearshift and saw that the car was now in neutral. I quickly put the car into park. I tried turning the keys to the ignition, and the car started up.

"What the hell was that?" I asked. "How does the car now suddenly work when it didn't earlier?" Tree said nothing.

"I think we should just go back home and try this another time," I suggested.

Tree stood there silently. Finally, he said, "I would like to know something."

"What?" I asked.

"How does a car move by itself *uphill* with no one pushing it from behind?" Sure enough, the car was pointing uphill toward the back of the cemetery.

I wasn't overly concerned with the cause of the strange occurrence—I just wanted to get out of the cemetery. We packed in the car and started out. As we got onto the path leading back toward the main road, a dog came out of nowhere and started running alongside the car and barking. Tree thought it would be funny to speed up and outrun the dog, but as he accelerated to a speed of 60 miles per hour, the dog stayed parallel with the car.

"What the hell?" he exclaimed. The dog kept barking and running with the car. Soon we approached the main road leading back to the highway and had to stop quickly to avoid going into the intersection. When we looked back to see if the dog was still with the car, it was gone. There was no dog to be found anywhere, not even on the road leading back to the cemetery. After this experience, we still felt getting back home was priority, so we continued on until we reached the highway and made our way back home.

Second Investigation: The Dog Returns

I returned to the cemetery with Phillip, Rachel, and Frankie over a year later. Phillip seemed eager to investigate the site, as he was intrigued by what had transpired during my last visit. We had driven up to the cemetery and pulled around back.

"Our first order of business is to locate Robina's headstone," I told everyone as we exited the car. I thought it was okay for the four of us to split up and walk throughout the cemetery individually to cover more ground. It was a large cemetery, but not so big that we couldn't see one another at all times; everyone would be easily accessible if something were to happen.

After about fifteen minutes, Rachel located Robina's gravesite. Not far from her grave was her father's headstone as well. We had our audio recorders running and started asking questions, giving moments of silence for a response from her or her father, George. We took EMF readings from the area around the headstones, but the devices did not activate.

Then, out of the corner of my eye I saw something move very quickly from right to left. This came from a distant area of the cemetery to the back left of where Robina was buried. I mentioned it to Phillip, who thought we should go check it out. We left the other two investigators with Robina and went to check out the area. It moved so quick that I honestly couldn't tell you if it was a shadow or something else. He and I walked the area, taking readings and asking questions, but we did not see or hear anything out of the ordinary.

After spending about two and half hours in the cemetery, it was time to go. We started back to the car as Phillip was talking into the audio recorder. "Dog continues to bark," he noted.

I looked back at him in confusion. I could not hear a dog barking, and Frankie gave me the same confused look. We thought maybe Phillip had hit a stage of old age in which he was thinking back to the golden days of dogs barking at the milkman making his deliveries. We said nothing to him and got in the car. As we were leaving, I couldn't help but look around and wait for the dog that followed my team to the main road on the previous trip to appear. We saw no dog and had no issues getting back.

About a week later we reviewed the audio and made some remarkable discoveries. First, there were numerous EVP from an unidentified female who seemed to be responding and reacting to Phillip. When we were investigating and Phillip was asking questions, he using a very loud tone and almost yelling. The first EVP we captured was the unidentified female saying, "Shut up!" There was a brief pause, and then in response to one of Phillip's questions she said, "Wait in the car!" The next EVP was simply a voice saying "stop" in the midst of dead silence (even sans the pump jack that was running).

The last was probably the most amazing of the bunch. On the audio, when Phillip comments on the dog barking, we could clearly hear a dog continuously barking in the background. All the other team members agreed that none of us heard a dog at any point during the investigation. But why was Phillip able to hear the dog so clearly and we weren't? Why was a dog not seen at any point during the investigation? Rachel suggested that the dog may be with the dearly departed that haunt the cemetery. But seriously, a phantom dog?

Is it possible that the dog was actually a spiritual protector of the cemetery? I know the area was Native American land, and I know there are spiritual beliefs about guardians and protectors of sacred areas. Perhaps the cemetery is one of those places.

Third Investigation: The Cows Aren't Watching

I made a return trip several weeks later with Tree and an investigator named Johnny. When we started making our way around the cemetery, Johnny noticed something in the distance. Two round lights appeared off in the distance as they were shining their flashlights toward it.

"It's a distant cow in the field," Phillip commented, but we soon discovered the lights were too far apart to be the eyes of a cow or any other animal. The next thought was that it was possibly a parked car or other vehicle, possibly left abandoned or with teens hiding out to fool around with one another. Then it was appeared that, again, the lights were too far apart. It was obvious that the two lights were moving farther apart over time. They were moving very slowly but definitely away from each other. By this time all four of us were watching the lights closely, only to see them move back together again. Phillip suggested that someone drive down in that direction and check out the lights at a closer vantage point. It wasn't long after his suggestion that we all watched the lights slowly dim and eventually fade out. They were gone, so we moved to Robina's grave.

We approached the headstone and placed Phillip's new EMF meter on the top. Phillip favored this device as it had a five-light LED setup much like the KII meter, but was larger in size, a darker gray, and had a better battery life. We took a few steps back from the headstone, and Phillip started asking questions.

"Robina, are you there?" The meter lit up.

"Can you see us?" he asked. Again, the meter lit up.

"Is your father here with you?" The meter did nothing.

"Are you saved, Robina?" Again, no response.

He continued on asking various other questions with no response. Then he asked, "Are you standing next to one of us?" The meter reacted. A few seconds later, Johnny walked from behind us to stand to our left. Tree (who coincidentally was standing under a tree) jumped back.

"What the hell?" I asked.

He stated that he thought Johnny was standing behind him, when in reality he was standing behind Phillip. Phillip and I looked at each other, noted the experience, and moved on. Nothing else happened after this point, so we decided to head home.

We reviewed the audio from this investigation to find more EVP directed toward Phillip. We recorded an unknown voice saying "Strange Phillip Holman" but not much else as far as evidence.

Fourth Investigation:
Dancing between the Tombstones

One night in 2010 my longtime friend and investigating partner Cathy and I were driving with Roy and John to an investigation in Mangum, Oklahoma, when our driver almost crashed us because he was seeing Chihuahuas in the road. Fortunately, we made it to the investigation okay and headed home after we had finished. Since we were so close to Arapaho Cemetery, I suggested we stop by. Everyone agreed, and we made the drive to the cemetery.

When we arrived, I saw the most awe-inspiring sight I had ever seen in a cemetery. The whole place was covered in fog—thick, dense, and everywhere. The only thing we could see was the street light from the road that illuminated the fog with an uncanny yellowish glow. We were all excited like children in a chocolate factory. We grabbed our gear and headed toward the middle of the cemetery.

I saw something and shouted for everyone to stop moving.

"Why the sudden request?" Cathy asked.

"I want everyone to stand still and focus on the middle of the cemetery." I saw a black mass rise out from behind one of the headstones, form itself into a humanlike shape, and take off running toward the road. I wanted to see if it would happen again.

Not long after, John exclaimed, "I see someone moving in the fog!" He was concerned that someone with malicious intentions was hiding in the fog waiting for us.

"Stand still. Turn off your flashlights, kneel down to the ground, and wait," I instructed. The only light source was the street light above.

Then Cathy said, "I see a figure running between the tombstones."

"Very slowly get up and head toward the front of the cemetery while trying to stay together," I said to the group. As we made our way to the front of the cemetery, we looked back, and I could see what looked like someone crouched down behind one of the headstones. At times, it would pop its head up and then back down. Cathy verified this as well. We spent about thirty minutes or so watching the shadow dance back and forth throughout the cemetery. Words cannot describe witnessing that type of phenomenon.

We did a ghost box session at Robina's grave. This is when we use a "spirit box," which is a small radio device that cycles through audio channels to allow spirit voices to come through and be heard. "Hello" was the only thing that came through that was clear. We started back to the car, trying to walk the path around the cemetery. John was walking by the headstones when he was suddenly tripped up. He looked down and found nothing that his foot could be caught on. He said it was something small yet solid in form. Thinking it was a brick or stone protruding from the ground, he started searching the ground but found nothing.

Fifth Investigation: Guardians of the Cemetery

About a year or so later, Cathy and I returned to Arapaho for another exciting adventure in the cemetery. We had friends Tiffany and Brittney, who had never had the opportunity to visit the cemetery, with us. We exited the car and made our rounds to different sections.

There were a few shadows spotted in some areas and a few words came through the ghost box, but the most amazing thing that happened this night was when we were leaving. We all packed into the car and made our way around the cemetery and out the main gate. As we were going down the road, I spotted something under the light pole that appeared to be crouched down. As we got closer to the pole, the "thing" started spinning around counterclockwise so fast that dirt was flying around on the ground. It then spread out what appeared to be wings and shot off into the sky.

I didn't get a clear look at it, but it almost looked grayish in color and almost had a faint glow to it. Cathy said she spotted the being before I had and watched it walk over to the location from where it took flight. She said at first glance, she thought it was a dog, but after watching it fly away she was convinced otherwise. To this day if you ask her, she'll tell you it was one of the most unexplainable things she has ever witnessed in her life.

This takes me back to the guardian theory. Was this possibly some spiritual guardian watching over us until we left? Or possibly watching over the cemetery to assure we did not cause any harm or damage? In either case, everyone in the car witnessed the being and noted this as the best experience we had in the cemetery.

Final Thoughts on Arapaho Cemetery

Overall, Arapaho Cemetery is still an active location and has a lot to offer the paranormal investigator. Being respectful of all cemeteries and the people buried in them is a top priority and can at times give you more of an advantage in getting responses from someone there who is willing to communicate with you. Whether or not the area is sacred to Native Americans, this will always be a "sacred" site for me. It was one of the most memorable and exciting cemeteries I have had the pleasure of visiting.

Chapter 12
RESIDENTIAL INVESTIGATIONS
Shawnee, Oklahoma

Over the course of my career as a paranormal investigator, I have had the opportunity to investigate many residences throughout the state of Oklahoma. A handful of these investigations have yielded great results. The cases you are about to read took place in the city of Shawnee, Oklahoma, and each one has its own uniqueness and mystery behind each one. Before we dive in, let me first give you a brief history about Shawnee.

Beginning in the late 1800s, Shawnee's development revolved around the railroad. In 1902, cotton and the railroad seemed to be the most profitable aspects of the small community. Over the course of the next hundred years, historic Shawnee made its mark on Oklahoma history by preserving its heritage and transforming into a thriving city. Many areas in Shawnee have a Native American presence, mainly Potawatomi, and continue to prosper today.

What is it that attracts so many spirits to Shawnee? There are rumored to be Native American burial grounds in multiple areas, and some say these contribute to the activity. Others believe that spirits are attracted to the land due to its spiritual energy. Whatever the cause may be, I have been to several places in Shawnee, Oklahoma, that have definitely convinced me that there was some sort of paranormal phenomenon.

The three Shawnee houses featured in this chapter were all sites that I examined for activity. The purpose of investigating these sites was not to "rid" the homes of spirits or give the homeowner valid reason to leave the property but rather to validate the haunting for the homeowner. Most of these places have had activity for many years, and they are still haunted to this day and always will be. Once you read these stories of actual occurrences, you too will agree that parts of the city appear to be a beacon to the ghosts of the dead.

The Haunted Doorbell Residence

The first and probably the most thrilling of these residences was a two-story home that was over a hundred years old. This was one of the first few houses I had investigated during my time with my first paranormal team. Once Phillip and I founded the group, we received several referrals for residential investigations in 2004.

I learned about this first house through a coworker of mine at the time. She informed me that her sister, Jennifer, lived in a house with activity and needed some professional assistance on how to handle the situation. I spoke with Jennifer on the phone, and she told me that there had been occurrences in her house that she felt were paranormal. She spoke of her husband seeing a figure at the front of the stairs and her children being frightened in their bedroom by an unseen force. An electronic doorbell mounted above the door outside the daughters' room would sporadically go off when no one was there. She also claimed to have a picture taken from outside the house of an unknown little girl in the window. I felt compelled to investigate the house, and yet I hadn't even seen it yet.

Jennifer and I scheduled a date for Phillip and I to come out to the house and conduct a preliminary investigation. A week or so before the date, I received a phone call from Jennifer's husband in which he explained that they would have to cancel the investigation due to one of their children being sick. I told him that it was okay and they should contact me back when they were ready to reschedule. Weeks passed, and I had forgotten about Jennifer and the case.

Then, I received a call late one night from Jennifer, asking me to come out to investigate the house due to the nature of the activity and the fact that it was getting worse. The girls were getting more frightened over the activity, and she was out of options. I could tell by her tone of voice that she didn't know what to do and desperately needed help. I couldn't come out that night, so Phillip and I planned to make the trip to Shawnee and do a preliminary investigation the following night.

Investigating the Haunted Doorbell Residence

Phillip and I traveled the next day to the house and met with Jennifer and her husband. Both seemed very nice and sincere about what they were experiencing. We took a few minutes to talk with them about what was going on to get more details and to explain what we were going to do. I asked if they would remain downstairs while we conducted a baseline sweep of the house to get familiar with the area. I told Jennifer that Phillip and I would come back tomorrow night and conduct a full-fledged investigation. She seemed pleased with the decision, and she and her husband promised to remain downstairs. We went upstairs to check out the girls' bedroom, where the activity was centered.

When we reached the top of the stairs, I went into the girls' bedroom, and Phillip went into the bathroom across from the bedroom. The girls' bedroom was very typical for a child's room. There were two small twin beds and various toys in the room. The bathroom was standard with tub and sink. I was preparing to take pictures of the room and had pulled my camera out of the case when Phillip started yelling.

"Logan, come into the bathroom!"

Puzzled about what he needed so urgently, I walked toward the bathroom. I could hear the Gauss Master EMF meter going off in the background. As soon as I entered, the atmosphere apparently went back to normal: the Gauss Master stopped going off. The temperature was normal, and it was very quiet. I approached Phillip from behind and looked over his shoulder. He looked very confused.

"I don't know what happened, but it was colder in here for a minute and the Gauss Master was activating, and now nothing is happening," Phillip said. He looked very convinced that someone or something had been in the room with him.

Jokingly, I sighed and said, "Oh well, whoever it was, I'll catch them tomorrow." I exited the bathroom and made my way back in the bedroom to take pictures. The sweep went as normal aside from that one unexplained occurrence. At the conclusion, I spoke with Jennifer and thanked her for letting us come out, and we decided on a time for us to return tomorrow.

"What do you think about the house? Do you think it's worthwhile to investigate?" Phillip asked as we were driving home.

"I felt something was going on, and the homeowners believed something was going on as well. They were convinced something was there, and most people don't get shook up over just anything," I told him. Phillip dropped me off at my house and returned home.

It was about twelve thirty at night, and before I went to bed, I got a call from Phillip.

"Do you remember the bathroom incident with the 'ghost' and what you said about 'catching it tomorrow'?"

"Yes," I replied.

"I have something you need to listen to."

"You mean you are already doing EVP work?" I asked.

Damn, he must not sleep, I thought. He played the audio recording of the incident, and right after I said I'd catch the ghost tomorrow, an old raspy voice said, "No, I'll catch *you* tomorrow." It very much sounded like an elderly man.

The next day I called and confirmed our investigation with the homeowner. Phillip picked me up from my house and had Claudia and Rachel with him, and we arrived in Shawnee just before eight at night. I met up with Jennifer, who I could tell was already uneasy due to what we experienced the night before. I was a little reluctant to tell her about the EVP we caught, but I felt it was my duty, given that I was the one investigating her house and I didn't want to leave anything out no matter how uneasy or disturbing it may be.

We started the investigation with two teams of three people: Phillip, Rachel, and Jennifer's husband were the downstairs team, and the upstairs team was Jennifer, Claudia, and I. We split up with two-way radios, and if any member of either team needed to go up or downstairs, they were to let the other team know.

We made our way to the top floor and immediately entered the girls' room. About thirty minutes after we started, we heard footsteps coming up the stairs.

"What the hell is he doing coming up here unannounced?" I muttered. Frustrated, I radioed to Phillip to ask him why he did not tell me someone was coming up.

"My team is in the kitchen and not anywhere near the staircase," he said.

"Stay still and quiet," I told him. "And please don't radio until I get back to you." The footsteps continued to the top floor until they reached the door to the room we were in. The door was cracked open about one inch and the hallway was dark. The footsteps continued, walking around the door. The spirit was either walking in a circle or back and forth, pacing the floor. Jennifer looked very frightened, and Claudia looked very confused.

I tried some interactive techniques. "Will you open the door and enter the room?" I called to the spirit outside. The door proceeded to creak open until it reached about four inches and stopped. I stared into the small, dark opening of the door halfway expecting to see someone looking in the room at us. Silence filled the room for five to ten minutes.

The footsteps resumed walking in a circle outside the door. I looked my team, who appeared to be frozen still and unable to breathe. I decided to take it a step further.

"Okay," I said. "If you can't open the door and come in, then I'm going to open the door and come out there." I got up off the bed and walked over to the door. I reached out for the old, round antique doorknob, and the moment my hand made physical contact with the knob, the doorbell near the bedroom started going off rapidly. Jennifer had seen enough. She got up from the bed, pushed me out of the way, and dashed out of the room. She frantically ran down the stairs to get away from whatever had followed us up there. I stood at the top of the stairs shining my flashlight and watching to make sure she didn't fall down the stairs in her frightened state.

As she reached the first floor and went into the dining room, I stood looking down the dark and empty staircase. Phillip came around and stuck his head over the railing and looked up at me to see what had just happened. Suddenly, heavy footsteps went down the stairs. The steps were very heavy and loud, much like those from boots. I knew there was no way anyone was on the stairs and what I was experiencing was indeed what I considered to be a ghost of the house.

Phillip simply looked up at me and asked, "You know there is no one on those stairs, right?"

I looked down at him and said, "I'll be right down."

We met back up with the entire team, and I explained what happened. Jennifer decided she was not going to leave her husband's side for the night, so the four of us investigators decided to conduct the rest of the investigation together. We made our way through the downstairs area of the house, including the kitchen. At one point, we were in one of the rooms in the back area of the house, and one of the investigators thought they saw someone run through the living room area of the house. We knew it was not the homeowners, as they went upstairs while we investigated downstairs. It was too fast for someone to get a picture, and we didn't have a stationary camera set up recording.

At the end of the investigation, we all felt we had gotten a few things out of the house that were positive evidence. We all smelt a woman's floral perfume, and at another point we smelt moth balls. Both smells seem to have manifested on the first floor of the home. The most compelling evidence we captured was the EVP. In addition to the old man, we captured another EVP unlike any other I had heard. It was something spoken in German. None of us spoke German and had no idea what it said. Phillip, trying to be smart, said, "I think it means 'something good man.'"

I presented all my evidence to Jennifer and told her to call if she needed anything more. Several months later, she called once again, reporting one of her girls talking about seeing a "yellow grandma" in the house. I returned with another investigator to the house but did not capture anything conclusive. I lost contact with Jennifer and her family shortly after my last investigation, though I would very much like another opportunity to investigate the home.

Final Thoughts on the Haunted Doorbell Residence

A year or so later I was speaking at a paranormal event held in Guthrie, Oklahoma. One of the topics we spoke on was EVP. I made the comment that we get all different types of EVP, including those in foreign tongues. I told the story of the German EVP I captured at the house and said we had no idea what it said. At the conclusion of the event an older woman approached me and asked about the German EVP.

"Do you have the EVP here?" she asked. I did not have it with me, but I suggested she visit our website and listen for herself. She said she would listen to it and see if she could decipher what it was saying and email me. I told her Phillip's theory of "good man" in hopes of that being able to help her.

She emailed me back several weeks later, writing, "That's not what is said." She confirmed that the EVP was in German and explained, "If you translate that into English, it repeatedly states 'I'm not dead, I'm not dead, I'm not dead.'"

I sat back and thought about what our research uncovered about the house. We learned through historical research that the original owner of the house immigrated to the United States from Germany. One parent was German and the other was French. He was also fluent in the German language. I believe that, for whatever reason, the original homeowner was haunting the home. I don't know why he chose to communicate with the girls specifically or where the perfume came from, but I know that there is too much evidence pointing to him in the home. Perhaps he cannot separate from the place he settled into and wants to share the house with whomever is occupying it at the time.

The Haunted Toy Truck Residence

Phillip and I received the next case as a referral from another paranormal team. This was also one of the first investigations that Phillip and I checked out back in 2004. We didn't know too many details about the house at the time but figured we would travel to Shawnee and see for ourselves.

Sherry, the homeowner of the residence, was a single mother of two children. She and her kids had been experiencing several types of phenomena. While most of the activity was typical for a haunting (shadows, voices, etc.), there was one factor that I found quite interesting. Apparently, her youngest child had a toy that operated on its own and would frighten him. The homeowner also reported seeing a young boy of Native American decent in the home. She said he was dressed in a white shirt and black pants. Phillip and I decided to make an appointment with the homeowner and get more details of the alleged haunting.

First Investigation: A Siren in the Night

After meeting with the homeowner, we spent a night monitoring the activity. I picked up the haunted toy, a monster truck, and made sure it was functioning properly and there were no defects that could be causing the toy to come on by itself. The toy appeared to work normally. The homeowner also claimed the toy would operate without the batteries. We took the batteries out of the toy and decided if there was any type of movement or noise from the toy, we could conclude there was something paranormal in nature going on.

The first night we decided to conduct a sweep of the entire house and then sit down in separate areas and document anything that might be going on. After the initial sweep, we sat in the living room area for a while and moved upstairs into the youngest child's room. The room was a good size with a small twin bed and closet. Various toys were scattered around the room, which had a distinct smell of wood. We put the battery-less toy truck on the floor in front of us. It was approximately 3:30 a.m., and I was extremely tired. I ended up falling asleep on the bed in the room while Phillip and the homeowner stayed awake. I was awakened around 4:20 a.m. when they decided to retire the investigation.

"Did anything happened while I was unconscious?" I asked.

"The truck didn't move, but it made a bizarre noise," Phillip explained.

"Did anything light up?" I asked, and he said no. We placed the batteries back into the truck and tried to duplicate the noise that he had heard, to no success. We packed up and started back toward Midwest City so he could drop me off. On the way, he played back the recording, which had the noise. The siren-like noise sounded drawn out and was preceded by two grunting noises.

Second Investigation: The Poltergeist Activity

During the course of about a month, we returned to the house with more team members and were not disappointed. Several different events transpired over our trips to the house. On one trip, we were doing research on the second floor of the home. Again it was late at night, and again I was extremely tired. Phillip and the homeowner were in the youngest child's room, and I decided to lie down in the hallway outside the room. I took my EMF meter and placed it at the top of the stairs. I activated the meter and left it standing up.

About sixty seconds or so went by, and I started to hear a very faint squelch coming from the meter. Now, keep in mind, this meter was reading on a scale of 1 to 10 milligauss due to the button not being pressed (which changes the scale to 0.1 to 1), so the range it was reading was somewhere between 5 and 8. I felt this was a high reading for being a random, out-of-nowhere energy. I looked up at the meter, which was maintaining a constant reading. I could not see the display of the meter in the dark. The squelch picked up and got louder. I could feel cold air slowly come up from the staircase. I sat up and continued staring down at the meter.

All of a sudden, I heard an audible *psssst* come from behind me to my left, and the meter took a flying leap down the staircase. I crawled over to the stairs and looked down. The meter landed about halfway down the stairs and was sitting a little over a step. I couldn't move. I know the meter could not have

fallen over and landed where it did. I also know it didn't fall
because I saw it take off in flight. Unfortunately, we were not
recording audio in the hallway. I quickly called to Phillip and
told him about what had happened. He seemed a little preoccupied, and I don't think he heard what I was telling him. I say
this because I retold him the story a day later and he freaked.
Whatever was there was very interested in communicating with
me and was looking to get my attention. It did a very good job.

Another event that took place in the home happened in
the living room area. The living room had two couches with a
tall bookcase. The bookcase had various items and pictures up
on top of it. There was a patio door leading to the back porch
of the home. I was walking around the living room with the
homeowner's teenage daughter, and I noticed that her picture,
which was usually displayed on top of the bookcase, was not
there today.

"Why did you take the picture down?" I inquired.

"We didn't move it," she said. My next thought was that the
picture had fallen over. I got a flashlight and stood on a chair
to see if it was lying on top of the bookcase. It was not. I then
looked behind the bookcase to see if it had fallen behind it.
There was no sign of the picture on or around the bookcase. We
went around the corner to the kitchen to ask the homeowner
about the picture disappearing. She claimed to know nothing
about it but followed us back into the living room.

When we all walked back into the room, and the picture was
sitting on top of the bookcase in the exact location it had always
been. I believe for a moment she thought Phillip and I were
trying to pull a prank on her, or maybe we thought it was gone
and it wasn't. I then explained to her about looking on and

around the bookcase for the picture. The picture never moved the subsequent times we went to the home.

Third Investigation: Hiding in the Dark

Another night while investigating in the living room, we experienced a strange set of occurrences. The homeowner, Phillip, and I were sitting on the couch. Phillip was looking around the room when he witnessed what he referred to as a "glowing orb" exit the air vent, float around the room, and take off down the hall. He and I got up and examined the air vent and hallway. At first, I thought it could have been an external light that came in through the window, but Phillip was adamant that it was a ball that came out of the vent. Nothing seemed to be out of place, and no one had a camera to take a picture. We returned to the couch and continued our investigation.

At one point during the investigation, Phillip jumped back into the couch. "A small child just took a step out of the doorway and backed up into it. It happened so fast that I couldn't make out much detail about what the child looked like or was wearing, but it was definitely a child, male with short dark hair," he said.

A few moments later I heard what I perceived to be footsteps going up the stairs. I walked around to the stairs and took a look around. I didn't hear or see anyone. I returned to the couch, where we finished the night's investigation a few minutes later.

Fourth Investigation: The Footprint

The homeowner called and claimed she had found a small, thin footprint on the rug in the upstairs bathroom. The bathroom was small with a rug in the center. The tub, toilet, and sink were all standard and intact. The footprint on the rug had a white, powdery substance that had hardened around the shape of the print. Phillip and I arrived moments later to examine it, and the first thing I wanted to do was measure the footprint to see if it could have been one of the kids. Unfortunately, we did not have the capabilities of collecting any type of toe print to examine closer, so I went to grab the measuring tape. The print was approximately six and a quarter inches long and about one and a half inches wide. Whoever or whatever left the print had a high-arched foot. We checked the kids' shoe sizes and didn't feel it would be conclusive to say it was one of theirs.

I then focused on the white powdery substance. I pulled a small rock of the substance from the rug with tweezers and went into the kitchen to examine it. First, I smelled the substance to see if I could identify any components, such as bleach, baby powder (which was my first guess), or soap. I couldn't smell anything distinct. I then crushed the rock into a powder. Still, I could not smell anything of familiarity. I carefully rubbed the powder together with my fingers, which were covered with a plastic glove. It had a very gritty texture and seemed to almost evaporate. I performed one last test with my specimen, taking a few small drops of water and mixing it with the powder. The substance blended in with the water and seemed to disappear completely. I was at a loss.

I have mixed feelings about the footprint. Although there were many things surrounding this home that we felt were paranormal, I don't know if this evidence was or wasn't. Either way, I couldn't draw a substantial conclusion about its identity.

Fifth Investigation: Unexplained Energies

Other strange things we witnessed in this residence were voices and EMF readings. One night our team—Phillip, Frankie, Rachel, and I—went out to the site. Frankie and Rachel were sitting downstairs in the living room of the home, and Phillip and I were upstairs examining the bedrooms more closely.

The homeowner's bedroom was the largest of the rooms. Red walls and a king-size bed seemed to fill the room. In the homeowner's bedroom, there was a small red box that for whatever reason gave off EMF. We could not find anything that would or could give off any type of electrical impulse. Yet every time we closed the box and put the Gauss Master to it, it would give off readings of 5 milligauss or higher.

Several minutes later, Frankie and Rachel heard children laughing. They claimed the sounds were coming from upstairs, but we didn't hear any laughing.

Final Thoughts on the Haunted Toy Truck Residence

Upon our last investigation, we learned that the homeowner was moving out of state. That was our final investigation, unless the new tenants request an investigation for themselves. I have not yet heard from anyone living there.

There are a few interesting footnotes to this story. One involves the monster truck toy. I asked the homeowner if I could take the truck for further observation, and she said yes. I put the truck in the trunk of my car and took it out a few times to see if I could get anything to happen. Keep in mind I never placed batteries back into the truck. I felt if the activity was paranormal, it could find another way to charge the car and activate it. I once heard someone say, "If you play with matches long enough, eventually something is going to burn." This applied perfectly to the situation that was to follow involving the truck.

I was exiting a parking lot one afternoon after completing an errand. I turned out of the parking lot and started my way into the intersection. As soon as I started to turn, the back seat in my car flipped down and the monster truck came roaring out from the trunk. It made its way from the back seat over the center console and onto the passenger-side floorboard. To make things worse, the truck was screaming "Gravedigger" along the way.

After avoiding several collisions, I stopped in a parking lot and called Phillip. I told him what happened and asked, "What should I do?"

"Go back to work," he said, "and don't worry about it." I looked down at the truck, now sitting in the floorboard. I felt safe just being parked and still in one place.

I picked the truck up and turned it over to open the battery compartment. *Who put batteries in the damn thing?* I thought. I disengaged the lock mechanism and pulled the cover off. No batteries. A few seconds later the wheels of the truck started spinning. I threw the truck back down to the floorboard, and it was laughing in a Joker-like voice that was programmed into it. I opened the car door, popped the trunk open, and tossed it inside.

I never again saw the truck activate or heard its disturbing voice: over the course of the next six months, the toy disappeared from the trunk. I don't know what fate the truck met, but I'm always waiting for the moment it busts into the room to make another appearance.

The Nine Spirit Residence

The third and final Shawnee residence I investigated was a two-story Victorian-style home that was a little more unique due to the nature of the activity inside. This home was owned by a medium named Carol. Her mother, Eileen, lived at the residence with her and was also a medium. I contacted the homeowner through a website that listed their plans to turn the house into a haunted bed-and-breakfast. I politely asked if our group could come in and investigate the home. They both agreed and were anxious to meet us.

Brandon and I first traveled to Shawnee and met with the mother and daughter mediums. They felt the presence of about nine spirits in the home, and the environment was violent and angry due to conflict over everyone sharing the same space. The spirits included a mean and spiteful school mistress; two young children, a boy and a girl; a servant girl; an older man known as Mr. George; two brothers, both middle aged; and a mysterious and violent man. Apparently, this was not the first time they had experienced spirits, but this was the most they had seen in one location before. Another alarming detail was the documented physical attacks. Most of the attacks seemed to be geared toward the homeowner. Carol had been hit, pushed down the stairs, scratched, and possibly choked. There was another individual who had been in the house and was also attacked. We took note of the activity and scheduled a time to come back to the house and investigate.

First Investigation: Initial Survey of the Nine Spirit Residence

Brandon and I went out to the house to take some video shots and get some ideas on how he wanted to shoot for the video. As we pulled up to the house, I could tell that Brandon was intrigued by the building.

I promptly showed him around the house, and my main area of interest was the basement. The basement was large, divided into two separate rooms. There were areas that appeared to be under construction because of boards set up to possibly build walls. There were concrete floors and minimal lighting throughout. It had a very dark feeling to it. The homeowners allowed us to go down into the basement for a quick sit-down. I don't know why, but I felt the house was particularly active that night.

We made our way through the basement, and Brandon asked me to go into the next room and see if I felt anything. I walked into the entryway and looked to my right. There was a large, slim figure standing right next to the doorway. It had uncanny human characteristics. Its head, for example, was very large, almost twice the size of a normal human head and oval in shape. It was like the character Stewie from *Family Guy* but not as wide. The face, however, was very small, with features much like a child's. The face was also very white, almost glowing. The long arms and legs just floated above the ground.

When I shined my flashlight toward it, it would go away. When I put the light away, and it would appear, much like the woman in the Guthrie hospital. I stood there for a very short time and returned to where Brandon was standing. I told him what I experienced, and he promptly took the IR thermometer and went to take readings. He found that the area where the figure was standing was colder than the rest of the room. He did not see the figure but documented the environmental differences.

We returned to the room near the stairs and proceeded to conduct a sit-down. After a while, Brandon got up to move, and I could see a dark shadow figure go around the side of him. As the figure turned around Brandon, the EMF array that was sitting on a table next to him activated. It appeared to us that once the entity went behind Brandon, it unintentionally activated the meter. We noted the experience and continued our investigation. Several minutes passed, and I looked up to see a shadow figure almost looking over Brandon's shoulder. Brandon turned around, saw the face of someone behind him, and jumped backward. I then told him I had not seen a face, just a dark mass.

After that experience, I think he had enough of the basement. We gathered our things and returned to the first floor, planning to take more time to go through the rest of the house, including the attic. We started on the first floor and then traveled to the second. There was one bedroom by the stairs we spent some time in, which was the room the kids were reported to be in. The room was small with a twin bed and closet. Several toys and childrens books were placed in the room to create the atmosphere of a child's room. As we started our communication process, we heard movement coming from the attic. There were sounds of something (or someone) being dragged across the floor. We then left the room and walked up to the attic.

As we entered the attic, I felt drawn to the back of the room. I didn't want to rule out any specific areas, so we made a sweep through the entire attic. As we neared the back of the room, I told Brandon to wait a few minutes to see if I could communicate with anyone. The room was completely dark. We then heard what sounded like static-like noises. After about ten minutes we decided to head back downstairs to conclude the evening. We told the homeowners that we would be back in the near future for an overnight investigation and headed back home.

Brandon, Penny, Albert, and I returned to the house on March 3, 2006, for visit that didn't have much in store for us.

A few shadows were seen in the basement, but for the most part it was a relatively quiet evening.

Second Investigation: Major Interaction

It wasn't until the second investigation that we experienced more significant activity. Our return came the following week on March 11, 2006. I arrived at the house with Brandon, Penny, Albert, and Jerico to set up for that night's investigation and decided to conduct video interviews of the witnesses and homeowners for accurate documentation of the events that took place.

As we were setting up for those interviews, something flew in from the living room and skidded across the floor. We searched throughout but could not find an item that would be capable of making the noise we had heard. Nothing was out of place, and as far as we could tell there was no way to further document the event.

We proceeded with the interviews and made our way into the living room after the filming. Brandon was sitting on the floor preparing the video camera for the initial sweep of the house. I notice a frustrated look on his face, and then a puzzled one. He was pressing several buttons on our video camera and looked confused about the functionality of the camera.

"What's your dilemma, Brandon?" I asked.

"I can't get the color night shot setting on the camera to go off," he explained.

"Try going outside the house and off the property," I recommended. He walked outside and onto the back porch, pushing the button the whole time.

"It's still not working," he said. I suggested he walk all the way off the property and try it. He stepped down the steps and onto the grass and as soon as he made it in the yard, the camera immediately switched settings. Dumbfounded, he made the necessary changes and walked back into the house.

"What just happened?" he wondered.

"I feel a definite energy on the property that was having a conflict with the camera due to it being electrical in nature." There had been other times in my investigative career when the camera and other electrical equipment had their battery sources drained or had malfunctioned. In addition, as he was sitting on the floor messing with the camera, something in my mind was telling me *go outside*.

We returned inside, and I took a seat in one of the chairs in the living room. Jerico joined me shortly to discuss the house.

Suddenly, we heard footsteps coming from the second floor of the house. We assumed one of the other members had walked up the other staircase and was looking around in one of the upstairs rooms. About the time the footsteps stopped, Penny, Albert, and the homeowner's mother entered the living room from the dining room. There was no way they would have had time to make it back through the back stairs in the kitchen before the noises ceased. Also, there was no one else in the house to make the noise. We explained what happened, and they stated they did not hear the footsteps or anything unusual. This was a good time to start the investigation.

Eileen gathered her dog and her things, vacating the residence for the night and leaving it to us. She made one last check to see if we needed anything and walked out the back door to head to her house, which was located next to the home on the same property. I didn't know if the absence of Carol and her mother would have an adverse effect on the activity, but I was willing to give it a try.

An eerie feeling came over me when I was in the house. The only way I could describe the sensation would be to say that it felt like someone was following me around everywhere I went. While I experienced most of this feeling in the basement, I also believed there was an equal amount of activity upstairs on the second floor.

We started the baseline sweep of the house and made our way upstairs and into the attic. It wasn't long before Albert started registering abnormal spikes on the EMF meter in different areas of the attic. There was an intense static-like feeling in the area, and I immediately surveyed the entire area of the attic. Albert was standing stationary, monitoring the spikes he was encountering. I focused on the area directly behind him. I could clearly see a child's shadow directly behind him to the left. I immediately notified everyone of what I was seeing.

The figure made a brief waving gesture with its left arm and disappeared. Jerico then described an electrical or static feeling. Although he was getting the strong feeling, the EMF was not activating at that moment. We heard sporadic noises throughout the attic in addition to several knocking noises, none of which could be confirmed as a natural source aside from a few that we determined to be external.

Next, we walked back down to the first floor to complete the sweep. The final section of the sweep led us back down into the basement. We entered the basement and took the usual readings. During the documentation, Jerico heard a child's voice. The strange thing is, the voice seemed to come from the other side of the basement, where I had seen the shadowy figure behind Brandon the first time I was there with him. Jerico claimed he didn't understand what the voice said, but it was clearly a child's. Hoping this was an indication that someone wanted to communicate with us, we conducted our first sit-down in the basement.

We grabbed the equipment and the arrays and made our way to the front part of the basement at the base of the stairs. We turned off all the lights and sat quietly. In the main room of the basement there was dim light coming through the windows. Almost immediately, we noticed shadow activity coming from the other room. The shadows would pass back and forth, come closer and then disappear, and remain stationary and then disappear. It happened so much, in fact, that we could not keep track of them all. It seemed that as time went by, they increased in number.

Several minutes later, the basement developed a very unpleasant feeling. I had felt it before at the abandoned church. It was the feeling of darkness overwhelming you, the feeling of being watched from every angle. The atmosphere became very uncomfortable very fast, and Penny and Albert decided they could no longer stay in the basement and returned to the first floor. The three of us who remained decided to move to the main area of the basement to continue our research. I couldn't help but remember the events that happened in there during my trip with Brandon, including the slim figure I had seen in the doorway. We continued the sit-down for another thirty to forty-five minutes and then regrouped with everyone upstairs to discuss our plans for the remainder of the evening.

We took a quick break and decided that we would conduct another sit-down, only this time in the "kids' room" upstairs. The kids' room is one of the many bedrooms on the second floor. This room in particular was decorated with toys and games especially for the two children spirits of the home. The homeowners referred to the male child as "Nicky" and the female child as "Charlotte." They told stories of how the children would run up and down the halls, slamming doors and turning the lights on and off. One story in particular involved Nicky and a marble that appeared in several areas of the home. They felt this child was placing the marble in different areas of the home to get attention.

After the break, we set up equipment in the kids' room and sat down. Earlier in the evening, Eileen entered the room and pleaded with the kids to make themselves known to us for the sake of scientific research, and I wasn't sure if that would have an impact on the activity or not. We all took a seat, with the exception of Jerico, who lay down on the bed. We started several communication techniques, including the use of toys.

At one point, I threw a jack down the hallway and asked if one of the kids would kindly bring it back to me. The jack never returned to the room. Jerico decided that he would try to relate to the children in a different manner, taking the father approach. With children of his own, I felt he would be successful at making a connection.

He invited the children into the room. "I'll tell you a story," he said. After about five minutes, he then recited the story of "Goldilocks and the Three Bears." Once the story had ended, he asked the children, "If you liked the story, will you make a noise? If you make a noise for me, I'll tell another story."

No sound was heard. We paused for a minute or two, and then he made another offer: "I want to play a game with you. It's like hide-and-go-seek. Make a noise around where you are, and I'll try to guess where you are. If I guess correctly, move to a different position, and the game will continue."

Moments later, Brandon starting having issues with the camera once again. The battery had drained significantly, and he was worried the camera would lose power. He switched the camera off momentarily to see what was wrong with it. During his examination of the camera, the doorknob to the closet in the room started moving. After a few seconds, we decided to open the door and see if there was anyone or anything inside that would cause the doorknob to move.

We pulled the door open slowly and stared into the darkness that was contained within the closet. Waiting for a screeching figure to come flying out at us with arms wide open, we sat there in silence and waited, but nothing happened.

Noises came from the hallway, several pops and taps at different times. I again asked the children if they would recover the jack and bring it into the room. I also stated, "If you don't want to come into the room, you could toss the jack in the room and remain in the hallway." The noises continued, and there was also a definite change in the temperature of the room: it got significantly colder over time.

Brandon was finally able to turn the camera back on. A little later, Penny saw what she perceived to be a female pacing back and forth in the hallway. We checked the hallway but found no one. At the conclusion of the sit-down, we decided to prepare for bed.

While Jerico and I dozed off into slumberland, Brandon, Penny, and Albert decided to head to the attic to film some footage of the reenactment segment of the video. We had been told by the homeowner and other witnesses that they had seen and felt the presence of a young man in his twenties who hung himself in the attic on a certain beam. Brandon, acting the part of the male, stood under the beam with a noose to re-create the hanging.

While filming, the investigators all heard a male voice grunt in one of the empty corners of the attic. They went to investigate but found no one. There were only two males in the attic area, and the other two in the house were asleep. They continued with the recreation of the hanging without any further incident. Not long after, they grabbed their equipment and headed off to bed.

In the middle of the night I awoke from sleep. I looked around the kids' room and listened to see if I could hear anything going on that might have awoken me. Everyone else in the room was dead asleep. I felt a strange sensation going down my leg as if someone were moving their hand down my leg. I then realized that nothing was touching my leg, but rather the sheet was being pulled off the bed. The covers traveled very slowly from the top of the bed to the bottom. I grabbed the sheet with my left hand and waited. Once the culprit saw that I had ahold of the sheet, it tightened up and stopped moving. I waited about sixty seconds.

I then took the sheet with both hands and pulled it as hard as I could. The sheet came flying back toward me, and there was a loud thump at the foot of the bed, as if someone or something were knocked over. One sleeping investigator moved briefly but did not wake up. I then heard a child's humming faintly manifest in the room. The voice, which appeared to be in surround sound in the room, now seemed to be loudest in the closet. I heard several other noises in the closet as well. They ranged from one or two knocks to things being moved around. The closet remained dark and the door remained closed. I had the urge to get up and open the door to see what was going on in there, but I fell back asleep.

The next morning we all awoke and went downstairs. The homeowners returned, and we talked to them about taking a different approach. We thought it would be a good idea to have some cameras stationed in the house. There were several areas we had in mind for a camera, but the only one that was convenient and easy was the basement. We set up one stationary camera in the area where I had seen the form behind Brandon. The camera remained in the home with twenty-four-hour surveillance and monitoring, with no positive captures.

Final Thoughts on the Nine Spirit Residence

I revisited the home a few times over the next few months and still found that there was activity. One night I was standing in the living room at the bottom of the stairs and began to hear doors slamming upstairs when no one was up there. I flew up to the top of the stairs to investigate but never found anyone. I also saw someone go down the back staircase, and I quickly followed them down. Once I reached the kitchen, I realized that I was alone in the house and no one had gone outside.

I believe the activity in the house was geared toward getting people's attention, as I feel they have much to say. While we didn't experience any violent activity, I do feel that it was a possibility for this to happen. I also could not at any point validate that there were nine spirits in the home or substantiate any of their given identities. I do know that there were multiple spirits in the home at many different times.

I'm sure many of you are wondering what happened to the house. The two mediums have since moved out, and the house sold to new owners. I have not been back to the house in several years, but if I got an email from the new owners complaining of restless spirits walking the house day and night, I would not be the least bit surprised.

CONCLUSION

As you reach the end of the book, you may have a few questions you want to ask. First off, did anything paranormal really happen throughout the course of this book? More importantly, how did we discover the existence of paranormal activity through our journey?

Well, we first need to understand what "the paranormal" actually is. The paranormal and paranormal activity, in a nutshell, are anything that happens that is void of any scientific explanation. Science comes into play when determining if these claims are truly paranormal in origin or if they come from natural sources, hence the investigation process. The only way (in my opinion) to conclude that something is clearly defined as paranormal is to thoroughly investigate a location—scientifically—and rule out any possibility of natural cause through process of elimination.

In every chapter, I have recounted personal experiences and shared evidence to indicate the existence and presence of paranormal activity, gathered through a variety of scientific equipment and techniques, and I've presented a wide range of paranormal experiences in haunted hotels, homes, and historic buildings throughout America's heartland.

Most of the places covered are famous locations (such as the Myrtles Plantation and Waverly Hills Sanatorium), but just because a place is known for being haunted does not guarantee it is actually haunted, nor does the reputation define what type of haunting is really present. One of the key differences in the hauntings is whether they are intelligent hauntings or residual hauntings. I believe that in most places we investigated there was an active, intelligent haunting taking place. In some cases, it was obvious through the nature of the experiences that we did establish communication with something there. In others, the experiences could have originated from a residual haunting or natural causes (e.g., external noises).

It is not uncommon for residual hauntings to include full-body apparitions, such as the appearance of people walking the halls of Waverly Hills. As former patients that once occupied the building, they could be residual hauntings. It is important to remember that residual hauntings are nothing more than atmospheric event playbacks from a time when the location was inhabited. Again, these events are often reoccurring and seen by multiple people; the woman falling from the roof of the Crescent Hotel is a good example. That does not mean the woman's spirit does not also inhabit the old hotel, however. It just means that one event was residual in nature and more than likely will be witnessed again in the future. I believe that in all paranormal experiences and hauntings, only 30 percent or less are actually residual in nature. The most common places to find residual hauntings are battlefields and prisons, due to the activity that surrounded these locations and the people involved with them at the time of their deaths. These places are also notorious for multiple deaths occurring at one time.

I would like to stress three simple things to people interested in doing paranormal investigations. Number one, above all, stay safe. Do not under any circumstance go out to a location, especially an abandoned location in the middle of nowhere, alone. Always tell people where you are going, and go with a group. Make sure you survey a location during the day to scout for possible obstructions or hazards that may be invisible in the dark. With that said, always make sure you have permission to be wherever you are. Do not trespass on private property or break into a location for the sole purpose of investigating. This could result in incarceration or worse. Number two, always research the equipment you are using. Doing background research will make you familiar with not only how devices work but also their purpose of use in the field. This will also allow you to eliminate any false positive readings that may occur along the way. Number three, always document your investigations thoroughly. Talk to any witnesses and keep a record of their statements. Make a log of the times and locations you capture readings. Make sure you back up any photographic or audio EVP that are captured so you will have them in case of data loss. The more positive evidence we have to present, the more conclusively we can say an area could be haunted. I believe the more evidence we have, the more the field of study will evolve.

I encourage anyone with interest of the paranormal to explore these and many other haunted locations throughout the country. I believe with enough investigation, research, and evidence, the evolution of paranormal knowledge will continue, and one day our questions of the unknown will be answered.

While this concludes the book, it does not mark the end of my studies in the haunted heart of America. With all the interesting places I've yet to investigate and the continuing advancement of technology, I'm excited to see where my next set of paranormal adventures takes me.

Acknowledgments

I would like to thank everyone who made this possible for me and helped me along the way, as I could not have done it without you and look forward to having more adventures with you down the road.

More specifically, I would like to thank Cathy Nance for the years of investigations and fun we had (looking for Lenny). I would like to thank former investigators Brandon, Albert, and Penny (Old Yeller) for making the trips with me and bringing along a sense of companionship. I would like to thank my current investigators Dale and Marleena for keeping me going and accompanying me on future investigations.

More so, I would like to thank my childhood love Ashley and my more recent love Danae. If it weren't for the both of you, I would have never known what it was like to fall in love with someone, and that kept me motivated and hopeful in the belief that with your love, I could accomplish anything. For Danae, I love you more than words could ever say. You are the brightest light in my universe, and I promise to love you until the end of time.

I would like to thank the site owners and managers who worked with me in completing this book. I sincerely appreciate all you have done for me.

As for the rest of my fans and followers, thank you for your support and encouragement as I continue writing these books. I will always strive to bring you the uncensored and undeniable truth about what the world of ghosts and the paranormal actually holds.

To Write to the Author

If you wish to contact the author or would like more information about this book, please write to the author in care of Llewellyn Worldwide Ltd. and we will forward your request. Both the author and publisher appreciate hearing from you and learning of your enjoyment of this book and how it has helped you. Llewellyn Worldwide Ltd. cannot guarantee that every letter written to the author can be answered, but all will be forwarded. Please write to:

Logan Corelli
℅ Llewellyn Worldwide
2143 Wooddale Drive
Woodbury, MN 55125-2989

Please enclose a self-addressed stamped envelope for reply,
or $1.00 to cover costs. If outside the U.S.A., enclose
an international postal reply coupon.

Many of Llewellyn's authors have websites with additional information and resources. For more information, please visit our website at http://www.llewellyn.com.

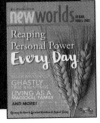

Author of *Haunted Asylums, Prisons & Sanatoriums*

JAMIE DAVIS WHITMER
with ROBERT WHITMER

America's Most

HAUNTED
HOTELS

Checking In *with Uninvited Guests*

America's Most Haunted Hotels

Checking In with Uninvited Guests

JAMIE DAVIS WHITMER

Journey into the mysterious world of haunted hotels, where uninvited guests roam the lavish halls, phantom sounds ring throughout the rooms, and chills run along the spine of anyone who dares to check in for a night.

Join Jamie Davis Whitmer, author of *Haunted Asylums, Prisons, and Sanatoriums*, as she explores nine of the most haunted hotels across America. From the Myrtles Plantation in Louisana to the Palmer House in Minnesota, these hotels are discussed in stunning detail, covering everything from the building's history and legends to first-hand accounts of paranormal activity that happened there. You'll also find photos, travel information, and everything else you need to plan your own visit to these haunted locations.

978-0-7387-4800-9, 264 pp., 6 x 9 $16.99

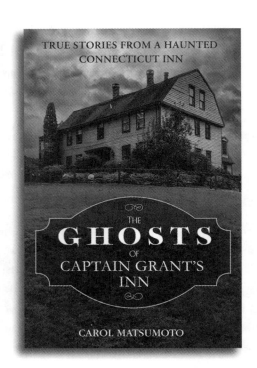

TRUE STORIES FROM A HAUNTED
CONNECTICUT INN

THE
GHOSTS
OF
CAPTAIN GRANT'S
INN

CAROL MATSUMOTO

The Ghosts of Captain Grant's Inn

True Stories from a Haunted Connecticut Inn

CAROL MATSUMOTO

Captain Grant's Inn is known by its guests as a spectacular destination for rest and relaxation … and encounters with friendly spirits! But this haunted bed and breakfast wasn't always the charming and accessible paranormal hotspot that it is today. In this book, Carol Matsumoto shares the fascinating story of how she overcame seemingly insurmountable challenges to renovate this historic Connecticut home with help from beyond the veil.

The Ghosts of Captain Grant's Inn is the true story of the miracles Carol continues to experience from the spirits who are connected to this enchanted place. From the beginning, visitors to the inn report unexplained occurrences and spirit sightings. When a ghost hunter uses dowsing rods to communicate with the spirits, a whole new era of discovery begins, with Carol and her friends and guests continuing to learn the fascinating stories of the twelve spirits who call the inn home.

978-0-7387-5302-7, 264 pp., 5¼ x 8   **$15.99**

To order, call 1-877-NEW-WRLD or visit llewellyn.com

Prices subject to change without notice

Exploring the Paranormal History
of America's Deadliest War

GHOSTS

—— *of the* ——

CIVIL
WAR

"Rich Newman's compelling new book . . . is the best way to visit over
160 spine-tingling haunts of this most tragic of American conflicts."
—JIM HAROLD, HOST OF *THE PARANORMAL PODCAST*
AND AUTHOR OF *TRUE GHOST STORIES*

RICH NEWMAN

Ghosts of the Civil War

Exploring the Paranormal History of America's Deadliest War

RICH NEWMAN

The Civil War left behind unforgettable stories of brave soldiers, heartbroken families, violent battles … and a paranormal legacy that continues to fascinate and scare us more than 150 years after the war ended.

Paranormal investigator Rich Newman presents over 160 different locations with reported supernatural activity related to the Civil War. Explore major battlefields, areas of smaller skirmishes, forts, cemeteries, homes, and historic buildings teeming with ghosts. Discover the rich history of these Civil War locations and why so many souls linger long after death. Featuring terrifying, heartbreaking, and captivating ghost stories, this book uncovers the supernatural secrets of America's deadliest war.

978-0-7387-5336-2, 336 pp., 5¼ x 8   **$15.99**

SPIRITS
OF THE CAGE

TRUE ACCOUNTS
OF LIVING IN A
HAUNTED
MEDIEVAL
PRISON

RICHARD ESTEP &
VANESSA MITCHELL

Spirits of the Cage
True Accounts of Living in a Haunted Medieval Prison

RICHARD ESTEP AND VANESSA MITCHELL

These examples are just a taste of the terrifying phantoms and tortured souls that dwell in the Cage, a cottage in Essex, England, that was used to imprison those accused of witchcraft in the sixteenth century. When Vanessa Mitchell moved into the Cage, she had no idea that a paranormal nightmare was waiting for her.

From her first day living there, Vanessa saw apparitions walk through her room, heard ghostly growls, and was even slapped and pushed by invisible hands. After three years of hostile paranormal activity, Vanessa moved out, fearing for her young son's safety. Then paranormal researcher Richard Estep went in to investigate. *Spirits of the Cage* chronicles the time that Vanessa and Richard spent in the Cage, uncovering the frightening and fascinating mysteries of the spirits who lurk within it.

978-0-7387-5193-1, 312 pp., 5¼ x 8 $15.99